100 THINGS TO DO IN SIOUX CITY AND SIOUXLAND BEFORE YOU DIE

Photo courtesy of George Lindblade

100
THINGS TO DO IN
SIOUX CITY
AND SIOUXLAND
BEFORE YOU
DIE

• •

LINDSAY HINDMAN

Copyright © 2020 by Reedy Press, LLC
Reedy Press
PO Box 5131
St. Louis, MO 63139, USA
www.reedypress.com

No part of this publication may be reproduced or transmitted in any form or by any means, electronic or mechanical, including photocopy, recording, or any information storage and retrieval system, without permission in writing from the publisher.

Permissions may be sought directly from Reedy Press at the above mailing address or via our website at www.reedypress.com.

Library of Congress Control Number: 2020937375

ISBN: 9781681062730

Design by Jill Halpin

Printed in the United States of America
20 21 22 23 24   5 4 3 2 1

We (the publisher and the author) have done our best to provide the most accurate information available when this book was completed. However, we make no warranty, guaranty or promise about the accuracy, completeness or currency of the information provided, and we expressly disclaim all warranties, express or implied. Please note that attractions, company names, addresses, websites, and phone numbers are subject to change or closure, and this is outside of our control. We are not responsible for any loss, damage, injury, or inconvenience that may occur due to the use of this book. When exploring new destinations, please do your homework before you go. You are responsible for your own safety and health when using this book.

DEDICATION

Dedicated to my husband, Zach, who introduced me to the wonderful area where his family has lived for over a century, and to my kids, Molly, Michael, and David, who help me see it through fresh eyes each day.

Photo courtesy of George Lindblade

CONTENTS

Preface... xii
Acknowledgments... xiii

Food and Drink

1. Start with a Donut from Jitters or Sunkist 2
2. Get Nostalgic About Burgers at Billy Boy 4
3. Have a Special Tea Party 5
4. Pick Your Own Fun 6
5. Scream for Blue Bunny Ice Cream 8
6. Gobble Down Flavor at the Iowa BBQ Company 9
7. Caffeinate at Siouxland's Best Coffee Shops 10
8. Taste the Wagyu Beef at Red Steakhouse 12
9. Sing the Blues and Eat Your Greens at the Blue Cafe 13
10. Go Dutch in Orange City 14
11. Delight Your Taste Buds at Diamond Thai 16
12. Treat Yourself to Tacos at La Juanita 17
13. Settle a Pizza Feud at El Fredo and Jerry's 18
14. Grab a Classic Dog at Milwaukee Wiener House 20
15. Twirl Your Spaghetti at M's 21
16. Believe in Broasted Chicken at Sneaky's 22
17. Indulge Your Sweet Tooth at the Sugar Shack 23
18. Devour the Best Pork and Steak in the World 24
19. Get Comfy at Udder Delights 26

20. Mosey to the Original Pizza Ranch. 27
21. Enjoy Historic Nightlife on Fourth Street. 28
22. Let Loose with Sioux City's Famous Creation: The Loose Meat Sandwich 30

Music and Entertainment

23. Try Your Luck at the Hard Rock Hotel and Casino. 34
24. Find a New Favorite Show at Lamb Arts Regional Theatre 35
25. Savor the Sioux City Symphony Orchestra 36
26. Observe Opulence at the Orpheum Theatre. 37
27. Rock and Roll with the Rockestra. 38
28. Enjoy the Classics at the Le Mars Community Theatre 39
29. Sing Along with the Sioux City Municipal Band 40
30. Cheer for Your Favorites at the Tyson Events Center 41
31. Put On a Show with the Sioux City Community Theatre 42
32. See the City from Grandview Park 44
33. Applaud the Lewis & Clark Theatre Company 46
34. Get a Song Stuck in Your Head at the National Music Museum 47
35. Praise with the Browns 48
36. Sing Along with Musicals from the New Stage Players 49
37. Come Ye to the (Woodbury County) Fair 50

Sports and Recreation

38. Stroll Along America's Longest River. 54
39. Start Your Engine at Park Jefferson International Speedway 55

40. Make a Splash at Siouxland Pools 56
41. Glide Downhill at Cone Park 57
42. Throw Your Best at Siouxland Disc Golf Courses 58
43. Jump for Joy at DropZone 60
44. Kayak to Your Campsite at Danish Alps 61
45. Take Me Out to a Sioux City Explorers Ballgame 62
46. Swing Low at Siouxland Golf Courses........................... 64
47. Reach New Heights at the Long Lines Family Recreation Center 66
48. Watch the Best at the NAIA Championships..................... 67
49. Hit the Ice at Siouxland Skating Rinks........................... 68
50. Enjoy Inclusive Play at Miracle Field 70
51. Wheel Around at Rollerama 72
52. Get a Low Score at Rush Werks or Yankton Bowl 73
53. Admire Riverside Trails at Adams Homestead and Nature Preserve .. 74
54. Get Spacey at the Fred G. Dale Planetarium 75
55. Toss the Pigskin with Stampede and Bandits Football 76
56. Hike More Loess at Stone State Park 78
57. Burrow Like a Badger at the Dorothy Pecaut Nature Center 79
58. Gear Up for Rev-Tac 80
59. Go Birdwatching at Ponca State Park........................... 81
60. Check (out) the Sioux City Musketeers 82
61. Fish and Relax at Southwood Conservation Area 83
62. Say Yes to Salix 84
63. Drive the Loess Hills Scenic Byway............................ 85
64. See What's Fishy at Gavins Point 86

Culture and History

65. Pay Tribute to Chief War Eagle. 90

66. Buzz by Bruguier Cabin 91

67. See the Safe in Calliope Village 92

68. Cruise America's Longest Roadway. 93

69. Twirl Around Windmill Park and the Orange City Tulip Festival 94

70. Do the Chicken Dance in Wayne 95

71. Pop into a Cute Little Museum 96

72. Remember the Past at the Flight 232 Memorial 98

73. Navigate to the Sergeant Floyd River Museum and Welcome Center . 99

74. Gaze Upon the Sergeant Floyd Monument 100

75. Play All Day at LaunchPad Children's Museum 102

76. Take an Expedition to the Lewis and Clark Interpretive Center 103

77. Soar at the Mid America Museum of Aviation & Transportation 104

78. Honor Law and Order at the Police Museum and City Hall 105

79. Don't Enter Any Raffles at the Peirce Mansion 106

80. Go Back in Time at the Sioux City Public Museum 108

81. Seek Serenity at Trinity Heights 109

82. Be a Connoisseur at the Sioux City Art Center 110

83. Rise Above It All in the Sioux City Skywalk System 112

84. Stay in Timeless Luxury at the Warrior Hotel 114

85. Admire Architecture at the Woodbury County Courthouse 115

86. Honor Heroes at Siouxland Freedom Park. 116

87. Follow the Captains to Spirit Mound 117

88. Venture into Vermillion's W. H. Over Museum. 118

89.	Experience Dakota Territorial History at the Mead Cultural Education Center 119
90.	Hike to History at First Bride's Grave........................... 120
91.	All Aboard at the Sioux City Railroad Museum 121

Shopping and Fashion

92.	Crunch Some Jolly Time Popcorn 124
93.	Find Your Fandom at Acme Comics 125
94.	Sweeten Your Day at Palmer's Candy 126
95.	Cross the Moat to Thinker Toys 127
96.	Aim for Briar and Bow 128
97.	Buy Some Bling at Thorpe and Company 129
98.	Find It All at the Marketplace on Hamilton 130
99.	Stroll Through Yankton's Meridian District 132
100.	Shop Local at Sioux City Gifts 133

Suggested Itineraries 135

Activities by Season 139

Index 141

PREFACE

Want to drive across the longest river in the US on the country's longest roadway? Or see the oldest cello known to exist, or the grave and monument for the only man to die on the Lewis and Clark Expedition?

You're in the right place.

Northwest Iowa is known for its amazing farmland, some of the best on the entire planet. But after you're done savoring a spectacular farm-to-table meal, you may be surprised to find how much else is lurking between the cornfields.

I'll share with you where to find the oldest popcorn company in America, how to stay in one of Al Capone's rumored hangouts, and where to find the largest public building designed in the Prairie School style.

I'll tell you some of the best ways to watch hawks and bald eagles soar over the confluence of the Missouri and Big Sioux Rivers, where Iowa, Nebraska, and South Dakota meet, and teach you about the history of this land, deep as the roots of the prairie grasses that adorn it.

After growing up in California, Missouri, and France, I came to Sioux City for college and unexpectedly fell in love with the people and the scenery. I've been to more than a dozen countries on three continents, but I'm proud to call Siouxland home. And I can't wait to show you some of the things that make it so special. Whether you're a lifelong resident, a first-time visitor, or somewhere in between, I hope you're inspired to expand your Siouxland bucket list and then have a blast checking it off!

• •

ACKNOWLEDGMENTS

I'd like to thank everyone who helped make this book a reality, but in particular:

Josh Stevens and the entire team at Reedy Press; George and Lou Ann Lindblade for generously sharing amazing photographs; Tim and Lisa Trudell for their advice; everyone who helped me with research, proofreading, and so many other parts of this process; and all of my family—especially my husband, Zach—who helped with proofreading, editing, research, driving me to many of these wonderful places and enjoying them with me, watching kids while I worked on this book, and so much more.

FOOD AND DRINK

START WITH A DONUT
FROM JITTERS OR SUNKIST

Jitters' specialty is a traditional cake donut with just the right hints of vanilla and nutmeg. Topping options include delicious frosting like chocolate, vanilla, and maple, as well as add-ons like peanuts, sprinkles, coconut every day and an ever-changing variety of seasonal and specialty toppings! Comfy couch seating and a cupboard of board games for customers to play make the experience as satisfying as the donuts. Also on the menu at Jitters are sandwiches, wraps, coffee, and tea.

Sunkist offers a wide variety of donuts, including the fluffy yeasted kind, jam- and custard-filled delights, danishes, and more. Sunkist's original location in the Morningside neighborhood is Sioux City's oldest still-operating bakery, with over 70 years of bread-, donut-, and cookie-making experience. Sunkist's new store on Hamilton Boulevard, adorably decorated with a sunshine-and-donuts theme, is Siouxland's only drive-through donut shop!

Jitters, 306 Virginia St., Suite D
(712) 255-9211, Facebook.com/JittersSiouxCity

Sunkist, 4607 Morningside Ave.
(712) 276-9422, Facebook.com/ForTheLoveOfReyes

Sunkist on Hamilton, 2519 Hamilton Blvd.
(712) 587-7856, Facebook.com/ForTheLoveOfReyesHamilton

TIP

Sunkist offers amazing donut holes that sell out every morning, so swing by early if you can!

GET NOSTALGIC ABOUT BURGERS
AT BILLY BOY

In 1962, all the coolest cats in Sioux City hopped in their hot rods to grab burgers and shakes at the groovy new drive-through called Billy Boy. The resulting parade of cars full of hungry people hasn't stopped yet. This locally owned burger joint still serves much of the same classic fast food as it did then: the burgers are perfectly simple, the fries just right, and the onion chips are out of this world. Finish your meal with one of the dozens of milkshake flavors. Look for seasonal items like fish sandwiches and chicken noodle soup. And Billy Boy's "shopper specials"—named after a bargain-filled section of the local newspaper—are one of the best options in Siouxland for feeding a crowd!

2328 Riverside Blvd.
(712) 233-1212

TIP
Billy Boy's location in Riverside makes it a perfect place to stop after fun at the Dorothy Pecaut Nature Center, Sioux City Railroad Museum, Sioux City Community Theatre, or Riverside Park!

HAVE A SPECIAL TEA PARTY

Get your pinky fingers ready! In the tea room at Special Teas for Special People in Dakota City, Nebraska, Siouxlanders are treated to dainty doilies, ladyfingers, cucumber sandwiches, and teas from all over the globe. Special Teas truly is "special" in the most traditional sense of the word—it's open only once each month for an extravagant themed tea party. Each party's theme both suits the party's occasion—from an "Irish Blessing" tea in March, to a "spring fling" tea in May, to a Christmas tea in December—and informs the party's every detail, from the decor, to the food and, of course, the tea! Each tea party at Special Teas for Special People has limited seating, available by reservation only.

120 S 13th St., Dakota City, NE 68731
(402) 241-0540
Facebook.com/SpecialTeasforSpecialPeople

PICK YOUR OWN FUN

Siouxland is home to some of the most fertile farmland in the world, and throughout the year, visitors and residents have many opportunities to celebrate—and taste!—the bountiful harvest that farmland produces. Every Wednesday and Saturday morning from May through October, you can find farm-fresh produce, meat, honey, and more at the Sioux City Farmers Market in the parking lot west of the Tyson Events Center. And while you're there shopping for the best farm products from three states, you can also eat at local food trucks, listen to live music, and enjoy community events, from bike-helmet giveaways to Halloween costume contests.

Other local farm-fun options include Lindsay's Flower Patch in Orange City, Iowa, where from May through September, you can buy pre-arranged bouquets of flowers or pick your own favorites fresh from the field. At Autumn Grove Apple Orchard in Sioux City, you can choose from more than a half-dozen varieties of luscious apples, which you can pick fresh off the trees. And at Scarecrow Farm in Lawton, Iowa, you can celebrate sunflowers in September or buy Halloween pumpkins in October—if you can find your way out of the epic corn maze!

Sioux City Farmers Market
101 Pearl St.
(712) 251-2616
FarmersMarketSiouxCity.com

Lindsay's Flower Patch
3750 470th St.
Orange City, IA 51041
(712) 577-2710
LindsaysFlowerPatch.com

Autumn Grove Apple Orchard
1658 180th St.
(712) 204-5951
Facebook.com/AutumnGroveOrchard

Scarecrow Farm
1592 Charles Ave.
Lawton, IA 51030
(712) 944-5644
ScarecrowFarm.com

SCREAM
FOR BLUE BUNNY ICE CREAM

Welcome to the ice cream capital of the world! Le Mars, Iowa, is the home of Wells Enterprises, the largest family-owned ice cream manufacturer in the United States, which makes Wells Blue Bunny ice cream. The Wells Visitor Center & Ice Cream Parlor is a charming ice cream eatery, steeped in history and full of the latest in frozen culinary creations. There you'll find an early 1900s-style ice cream counter with 40 flavors of Blue Bunny ice cream, including two parlor exclusives: huckleberry and mocha almond fudge. You can also try sorbets, sherberts, ice cream sandwiches, Bomb Pops, bunny-shaped sugar cookies, and much more! The parlor's ground floor also features meeting space and a gift shop with everything from handcrafted ceramic ice cream bowls to plush blue bunnies and tie-dyed Bomb Pop shirts. Upstairs, wall art that's as informative as it is decorative showcases the history of ice cream, while visitors enjoy not only their frozen treats but also interactive fun for kids and an ice-cream-themed movie theater!

115 Central Ave. NW
Le Mars, IA 51031
(712) 546-4522
ILoveWells.com

GOBBLE DOWN FLAVOR
AT THE IOWA BBQ COMPANY

Picture a plate of sizzling-hot pork ribs and brisket, dripping with sauce. Now fill up that plate in your mind with some potato salad, beans, coleslaw, mac and cheese, cornbread, green beans, and jalapeño poppers. Are you drooling yet? You will be when you see it, smell it, and (best of all) taste it at the Iowa BBQ Company in Le Mars. All the ingredients are locally sourced, including the all-natural antibiotic-, hormone-, and additive-free heritage-breed pork. Iowa raises the most hogs in America, and Iowa BBQ Company accepts only the best of the best! The company's custom smoker burns Midwest red oak, and every bit of each of its meals is handmade from scratch. Besides the delicious meals available every day, Iowa BBQ Company also offers special seasonal fare, like smoked turkeys for Thanksgiving. No wonder they're always winning awards for best barbecue! Iowa BBQ Company is sure to spice up your time in Siouxland.

100 Plymouth St. W
Le Mars, IA 51031
(712) 541-6606
IABarbeque.com

CAFFEINATE
AT SIOUXLAND'S BEST COFFEE SHOPS

Coffee in Iowa is much more than just a group of silver-haired farmers enjoying their morning cup of joe on a peaceful porch—although there is plenty of that, too! Sample the Siouxland coffee scene and find whatever your inner coffee lover is seeking. Stone Bru, in Sioux City, Iowa, and Dakota Dunes, South Dakota, offers an organic coffee that won the 2020 Siouxland Choice Awards for best coffee. At Hardline Coffee in downtown Sioux City, you'll find live indie music, shelves full of used books, and community events like board game nights. Pierce Street Coffee Works in Sioux City shines with eclectic decor and a creative sandwich menu; regulars recommend the curry chicken salad. At Hawks Coffee Shop in Sergeant Bluff, you can enjoy gourmet cupcakes and cookies from local bakers and take part in crafty events like decorative sign painting. For an experience a bit closer to the idyllic stereotype mentioned above, try Movillatte in Moville, where the beautiful rural view along the old historic US Highway 20 stretches for miles, and where the eponymous Movillatte—a chocolatey caramel creation—is as suited for Instagram as for the cornfield. Or head to Koffie Knechtion for coffee and treats, with a side of live music in the pasture and a stay in their treehouse Airbnb!

Pierce Street Coffee Works
1920 Pierce St.
(712) 255-1226

Hardline Coffee
611 Fifth St.
HardlineCoffeeCo.com

Hawks Coffee Shop
110 Gaul Dr.
Sergeant Bluff, IA 51054
(712) 271-2007
HawksCoffeeShop.com

Koffie Knechtion
419 Golf Rd.
South Sioux City, NE 68776
(712) 635-7374
Facebook.com/TheKoffieKnechtion

Movillatte
503 Frontage Rd.
Moville, IA 51039
(712) 873-5550
Facebook.com/Movillatte

Stone Bru
4243 Gordon Dr.
(712) 281-4242
Facebook.com/StoneBru

Stone Bru Dunes
400 Gold Circle
Dakota Dunes, SD 57049
(712) 281-4242
Facebook.com/StoneBruDakotaDunes

TASTE THE WAGYU BEEF
AT RED STEAKHOUSE

At Red Steakhouse in Vermillion, South Dakota, enjoy a dining experience which effortlessly combines a casual atmosphere with sophistication and elegance. The menu offers something for every diner, from relaxed lunch options, to classic steaks and potatoes, to inventive and impressively plated upscale fare, all exquisitely prepared by Chef Christopher Eldred and his team. Without a doubt, a star of the show at Red Steakhouse is the gourmet Wagyu beef, produced by Siouxland farmers Brad and Shawna Feddersen of Anthon, Iowa. Wagyu beef comes from a Japanese breed of cattle, and is known for its unique and superb marbling and flavor. Red Steakhouse also has a dedicated keto menu, so no need to choose between excellent fine dining and your health goals. While you're eating, make sure to glance around the historic building, which First National Bank and Trust originally built in 1939. The old bank vault is still in use, but instead of securing the cash, it now holds the fine wine!

1 E Main St.
Vermillion, SD 57069
(605) 624-0079
TheRedSteakhouse.com

SING THE BLUES AND EAT YOUR GREENS
AT THE BLUE CAFE

Visitors to the Blue Cafe walk away feeling anything but blue. The Blue Cafe is on the same block as the Sioux City Conservatory of Music and the Gimme Shelter Anti-Mall vintage store, and all share an owner. Both businesses on "the Block" financially support the efforts of the conservatory, and conservatory students frequently perform at the Blue Cafe, to the delight of diners. The Blue Cafe has hosted hundreds of intimate concerts on its cheerful corner stage, and also hosts other events, from wine tastings to open-mic nights. The cozy cafe offers limited seating in a bright, stylish environment that's totally social media ready, while its fresh ingredients and upscale fare leave visitors raving about the food itself, especially the pizza, the salads, and the omelettes. Whether you're there to listen to the blues, to take the stage yourself, or for the blueberry pie, you'll leave the Blue Cafe feeling nourished!

1301 Pierce St.
(712) 574-1751
Facebook.com/1301BlueCafe

GO DUTCH
IN ORANGE CITY

Orange City, Iowa was founded by immigrants from Holland in the late 1800s, and they brought with them a proud Dutch heritage which still pervades the community today. That includes Dutch heritage of the culinary variety, which really shines at Dutch Bakery. Don't let the understated name or appearance fool you: Dutch Bakery is a baking powerhouse, using high-end baking techniques based on traditional European methods. Dutch Bakery serves a variety of donuts and other baked goods, but is most famous for its Dutch letters (a delicious pastry), almond patties, and other European style-pastries. And kids rave about Dutch Bakery's pink bear cookies!

For another Dutch-flavored experience, head to the Little White Store, Orange City's oldest retailer, where the Dutch Heritage Boosters sell poffertjes (a puffy gourmet cousin to silver dollar pancakes) on special occasions. At Brad's Breads and Bakery, also in Orange City, you'll find all kinds of artisan bread and baked goods, including many created by owner Brad Gabel, based on a secret recipe passed down from his uncle. All of Brad's delicious wares are baked and sold exclusively in Sioux County.

However you split the bill in Orange City, you'll be glad you went Dutch.

Dutch Bakery
221 Central Ave. NE
Orange City, IA 51041
(712) 737-4360

The Little White Store
123 Central Ave. NE
Orange City, IA 51041
DutchHeritageBoosters.com

Brad's Breads and Bakery
101 Central Ave. NE
Orange City, IA 51041
(712) 707-9170
BradsBreadsOC.com

DELIGHT YOUR TASTE BUDS
AT DIAMOND THAI

Locals hail Diamond Thai as one of the best culinary surprises in Siouxland—authentic Thai cuisine that's as good as or better than anything you can find in America's biggest cities. Opened by a Vietnamese immigrant, the restaurant was recently acquired by a Laotian American husband-and-wife team who continue to offer the most popular authentic Thai dishes from Diamond Thai's original menu, and have also added their own Laotian flavors and foods. Whatever you order, be sure to include a side of spring rolls with their signature peanut sauce! Diamond Thai is also a particular favorite of Siouxland vegans.

515 W Seventh St.
(712) 258-2343

TREAT YOURSELF TO TACOS
AT LA JUANITA

For authentic Mexican food, La Juanita Taqueria is Siouxland's best bet. In fact, La Juanita is one of the best bets for Mexican food in America. Its burrito has won frequent national recognition as one of the 10 best in the country, including by some very influential national magazines, and has even been described as "life-changing." The near-northside location, just past downtown Sioux City, is wonderfully cozy, with an open-kitchen plan where you can watch the burrito-making masters in action. And the food speaks for itself—the burritos, but also the tacos, chimichangas, enchiladas, and so much more—as does the willingness of customers to wait for it in a line that's out the door on a daily basis! Owner Christina Bautista (who named the restaurant after her sister) and her team use fresh, high-quality ingredients to produce world-class Mexican food. Be sure to grab a glass-bottle Mexican Coke (with real sugar—no high-fructose corn syrup here!) or a Jarritos from the cooler to complete the experience!

1316 Pierce St.
(712) 279-0772

SETTLE A PIZZA FEUD
AT EL FREDO AND JERRY'S

Sioux City's first pizzeria, El Fredo, was opened in 1957 on the west side in 1957 by its namesake, WWII veteran Fred Lennon, whose family still runs this Siouxland culinary staple. El Fredo is known for made-to-order pizzas with risen crusts, fresh toppings, and especially its slightly sweet but delightfully zesty sauce. Today, El Fredo has two locations in Sioux City and a third location in Vermillion which opened in 2020.

Across town in the Morningside neighborhood, Jerry and Ilene Foisters opened a second pizzeria, Jerry's, in 1959. Jerry and Ilene's grandchildren and great-grandchildren are still running the restaurants today, and the pizzas are as good as ever. Jerry's is famous for its traditional thin crust, piled high with more toppings than you would believe could fit on a pizza!

Having these two great pizzerias, of course, set off a now decades-long friendly debate among Siouxland pizza-lovers over which of these two family-owned franchises has the best pizza. To this day, no consensus has been reached, except that both are delicious! Whichever you choose, make sure to place your order early—El Fredo and Jerry's can get pretty busy on Friday and Saturday nights, but it is *always* worth the wait.

El Fredo Pizza
523 W 19th St.
(712) 258-0691
Facebook.com/ElFredoPizza

Jerry's Pizza
1417 Morningside Ave.
(712) 276-1359
JerrysPizzaSiouxCity.com

GRAB A CLASSIC DOG
AT MILWAUKEE WIENER HOUSE

Milwaukee Wiener House in Sioux City is a great example of a simple concept done better than you ever thought possible. At Milwaukee Wiener, the usually humble hot dog is elevated to an art form: perfectly cooked, slathered with the perfect homemade chili, onions, and other fresh ingredients, and served with a side of nostalgia. Milwaukee Wiener House opened in 1918, originally on Fourth Street, and took its name not from the city in Wisconsin but from the nearby Milwaukee Railroad tracks. Today the restaurant is owned by a pair of brothers whose pride, passion, and love for the history of their restaurant is apparent in every detail—from the memorabilia on the walls, to their great T-shirts, to the vintage gas grill they use to cook their Coney-style dogs.

301 Douglas St.
(712) 277-3449
Facebook.com/MilwaukeeWiener

TWIRL YOUR SPAGHETTI
AT M'S

Head to M's in Sioux City for traditional Italian fare and an upscale but cozy candlelit ambience. M's features a delicious fine-dining experience by Chef Melis Spencer, one of the founding members of the American Culinary Federation of Siouxland. Spencer and her team at M's are best known for gourmet pasta dishes, from chicken fettuccine alfredo to lobster pappardelle, as well as incomparable appetizers like lavish charcuterie plates and mussels in garlic wine sauce. M's also offers one of Siouxland's most extensive wine lists, available from the M's Underground wine cellar. M's also has its own attached wine store, M's Uncorked. Formerly known as Luciano's, M's has been a Siouxland staple for over 20 years—not just for authentic Italian cuisine, but also as one of the best romantic dinner spots around!

1021 Fourth St.
(712) 258-5174
MsOn4th.com

BELIEVE IN BROASTED CHICKEN
AT SNEAKY'S

There's nothing sneaky about what makes Sneaky's Chicken so good: it's the broasted chicken! Broasting, a uniquely Midwestern method of preparing chicken which combines deep frying and pressure cooking, takes fried chicken to a whole other level. And Sneaky's Chicken in Sioux City, opened by brothers Dave and Rick Ferris in 1979, does broasted chicken better than anyone—which is why theirs is often recognized as some of the best chicken in Iowa. At Sneaky's, you'll always find perfectly tender chicken with crispy golden skin, along with all of the delicious sides you would expect: broasted potatoes, potato wedges, coleslaw, baked beans, and more. And although chicken is definitely the star of the menu, Sneaky's offers other down-home comfort food like ribs, patty melts, and burgers. And don't miss the lunch buffet! Just look for the sign with Sneaky's adorable mascot, Sneaky the Raccoon!

3711 Gordon Dr.
(712) 252-0522
SneakysChicken.com

INDULGE YOUR SWEET TOOTH
AT THE SUGAR SHACK

A peek at the counter of the Sugar Shack Bakery in Sioux City is like going behind the scenes of a reality baking show, with Pinterest-worthy cookies, cakes, and other confections that look like works of art and taste even better than they look. Sugar Shack, best known for its amazing sugar-cookie bouquets, great for any occasion, is also the best place in Siouxland for gourmet cakes for weddings or any other reason! The bakery offers a variety of flavors, from classics like chocolate and vanilla to trendier options like pink champagne and tres leches, as well as luscious buttercream and whipped toppings and dozens of filling options like caramel mousse and chocolate ganache. Sugar Shack Bakery has won myriad local, regional, and national awards, and it's easy to see why!

700 Jennings St.
(712) 252-5598
TheSugarShackBakery.com

DEVOUR THE BEST PORK AND STEAK IN THE WORLD

Siouxland is farm country, with some of the best farmland in the world, not just for growing corn, but also for raising hogs, beef cattle, and lambs. The area's renowned steakhouses and burger joints make prime use of the sublime meat that local farmers produce. With its wonderful view of the Missouri River, Kahill's Chophouse in South Sioux City, Nebraska, combines the casual and the elegant with the best locally sourced ingredients for a classic steakhouse experience. Don't miss the prime rib Sunday brunch! Archie's Waeside in Le Mars, Iowa, won the America's Classic award from the James Beard Foundation, which described Archie's as "a citadel of American beef cookery." Archie's has also been recognized by *Rachel Ray* magazine and earned many other awards and accolades, as well as the love of its Siouxland regulars. The Golden Pheasant steakhouse, just east of Remsen, Iowa, is a hidden treasure which many locals argue serves the best filet in Siouxland. The Lawton Exchange serves up classics like pork tenderloins, burgers, and creative specials, all done farm-to-table style. And Table 32 offers upscale craft food and drinks, along with Siouxland's best dedicated gluten-free menu. There's no way to go wrong with the best meat in the world!

Kahill's Chophouse
385 E Fourth St., #1750
South Sioux City, NE 68776
(402) 494-5025
Kahills.net

Archie's Waeside
224 Fourth Ave. NE
Le Mars, IA 51031
(712) 546-7011
ArchiesWaeside.com

Golden Pheasant
44028 Highway 3
Remsen, IA 51050
(712) 786-9455
Facebook.com/GoldenPheasantSteakhouse

The Lawton Exchange
311 Cedar St.
Lawton, IA 51030
Facebook.com/TheLawtonExchange

Table 32
100 Virginia St.
(712) 454-1866
TableThirtyTwo.com

GET COMFY
AT UDDER DELIGHTS

Udder Delights, a diner and ice cream shop in Wayne, Nebraska, features wonderful made-from-scratch traditional diner fare: Nebraska-raised buffalo burgers, homemade apple pie, and all-day breakfast featuring classics like biscuits and gravy. But the undeniable star of the menu is the ice cream. The variety of syrups and add-ons is expansive—stop by for one-of-a-kind ice cream treats like the "Car Wash," vanilla ice cream swirled with fresh homemade brownies and hot fudge! Of special note is the famous "drunken udder" menu for the over-21 crowd. Service is fast and cheery, in the Midwest-nice style. And you're welcome to sit and play the board games that line the windowsills while you dine!

209 E Seventh St.
Wayne, NE
(402) 375-1855
Facebook.com/Udder-Delights-1765828680156997

MOSEY TO THE ORIGINAL PIZZA RANCH

Pizza Ranch, with over 200 locations in more than a dozen states, is a Siouxland (and Midwestern) institution. It all began in 1981 in Hull, Iowa, when a teenager started the original location with the help of a loan from his parents (who saw the potential in his idea and helped him come up with his Western theme). Today, Pizza Ranch is famous for its buffet, which features almost any kind of pizza you can imagine (make a request!), some of the best fried chicken around, and outstanding desserts like buttery, frosted Cactus Bread and fruit-topped dessert pizzas. The regional chain offers delivery and carryout, and has recently added new arcades at locations in Sioux City and Vermillion, South Dakota. Along with the exciting new locations, the original location is still going strong in founder Adrie Groeneweg's hometown of Hull.

1015 Main St.
Hull, IA 51239
(712) 439-1853
PizzaRanch.com

ENJOY HISTORIC NIGHTLIFE
ON FOURTH STREET

When it comes to drinks, dining, and fun, Historic Fourth Street is the heart of downtown Sioux City. Historic Fourth Street is home to some of Siouxland's best bars and restaurants, housed in over a dozen buildings that date to the late 1800s. Many of the buildings are architecturally significant examples of the Richardsonian Romanesque style, and two—the Evans Block and Boston Block—are listed on the National Register of Historic Places. When the sun is shining, visitors to Historic Fourth Street can grab a bite to eat while shopping the many delightful antique stores. Everything is within easy walking distance of everything else, so you can eat and explore to your heart's content. And if you get tired, sit and enjoy the view in the courtyard at Fourth and Pierce Streets or in the fountain-filled plaza at Fourth and Virginia Streets next to the Promenade Theatre.

> **TIP**
> Historic Fourth Street is home to many of Siouxland's community parades, most notably a parade celebrating St. Patrick's Day and a holiday lights parade that culminates when Santa Claus lights up the community Christmas tree in front of the Sioux City Public Museum.

Rebo's
Mexican and American food
1107 Fourth St.
(712) 560-4144
Facebook.com/
Rebos-120006824683078

Marto Brewing Co.
Brewery and pizzeria
930 Fourth St.
(712) 560-3397
MartoBrewing.com

The Diving Elk
Upscale restaurant and bar
1101 Fourth St.
(712) 234-0000
Facebook.com/TheDivingElk

1008 Key Club
Speakeasy
1008 Fourth St.
(712) 255-5973
Facebook.com/1008KeyClub

The Marquee
Music venue and bar
1225 Fourth St.
(712) 560-4288
TheMarqueeLive.com

The Promenade
Movie theater
924 Fourth St.
(712) 277-8300
MainStreetTheatres.com/
SiouxCity.html

Soho Kitchen
Modern American restaurant and bar
1024 Fourth St.
(712) 258-3434
SohoSiouxCity.com

Brightside Cafe
Breakfast and lunch
525 Fourth St.
(712) 224-7827
SiouxCityBrightside.com

Buffalo Alice
Restaurant and bar that goes by B.A.'s
1022 Fourth St.
(712) 255-4822
BuffaloAlice.com

LET LOOSE WITH SIOUX CITY'S FAMOUS CREATION:
THE LOOSE MEAT SANDWICH

Whether you call it a tavern, a Charlie Boy, a Maid-Rite, or simply a loose meat sandwich, it's Sioux City's culinary claim to fame. The savory sandwiches are Siouxland's must-try meal if you're just passing through and a delicious staple for those who lived here. Local legend says that the loose meat sandwich was invented in Sioux City in 1924, possibly at Ye Olde Tavern or Miles Inn. Although the precise blend of spices and combination of garnishes varies from maker to maker, every loose meat sandwich—whatever its name—includes the same essential elements: fresh ground beef, lightly seasoned (maybe with ketchup, garlic, or horseradish) and cooked loose rather than in a patty, served on a warm, fluffy hamburger bun with simple toppings (like mustard, a pickle, a few onions, or even a slice of cheese) that highlight the sandwich's simple goodness. Try it as a "Charlie Boy" at Miles Inn, or as a "tastee" at Tastee Inn & Out, or as a "loose meat" at one of Siouxland's other great eateries. Better yet, try them all!

Former "Ye Olde Tavern"
1322 Jackson St.

Tastee Inn & Out
2610 Gordon Dr.
(712) 255-0857
TasteeInnAndOut.com

Miles Inn
2622 Leech Ave.
(712) 276-9825

Bob's Drive Inn
23 Fifth Ave. SW
Le Mars, IA 51031
(712) 546-5445

Photo courtesy of George Lindblade

MUSIC AND ENTERTAINMENT

TRY YOUR LUCK
AT THE HARD ROCK HOTEL AND CASINO

Sioux City got a whole lot more rockin' when the Hard Rock Hotel & Casino came to downtown Sioux City. The casino gaming floor has over 800 slot machines and dozens of gaming tables, and upstairs you'll find one of Sioux City's best hotels. The Hard Rock's restaurants Main + Abbey, World Tour Buffet, and Fuel American Grill will delight your taste buds, while the Yards and Lobby Bar is a great place to hang out for a drink. Of course, Hard Rock has decorated the whole place with their signature rock music memorabilia, plus a gift shop so you can score your own swag. You can also catch a show at Anthem, an intimate indoor stage. Worthy of special mention is Battery Park, the Hard Rock's outdoor concert venue, which brings world-class music acts to Siouxland.

111 Third St.
(712) 226-7600
HardRockCasinoSiouxCity.com

FIND A NEW FAVORITE SHOW
AT LAMB ARTS REGIONAL THEATRE

Since 1979, Lamb Arts Regional Theatre in Sioux City has been staging professional theater productions for Siouxland audiences, featuring works ranging from Shakespeare to edgy modern plays to works by local playwrights, including two world premieres. Lamb is also known for the Lamb School of Theatre & Music and high-quality children's shows, regularly performed for area students by the professional company and the students in the Lamb school.

Lamb is renovating a historic auditorium at 625 Douglas Street. The building, constructed in 1909, has previously been a legion hall, a ballroom, and a television studio. Once fully restored, the theater will be Lamb's permanent home for performances and theater education, featuring multiple stages, classrooms, a cabaret-style bar, and flexible event space, all of which will allow Lamb to continue enriching the arts in Siouxland.

(712) 255-9536
LambTheatre.com

SAVOR THE SIOUX CITY SYMPHONY ORCHESTRA

Beethoven. Puccini. Freddie Mercury. The Sioux City Symphony Orchestra brings the musical works of these masters—and many others—to the people of Siouxland! Performing regularly at the Orpheum Theatre under the direction of Ryan Haskins, the talented local musicians wow Sioux City audiences with a wide variety of music, from the expected classical pieces to the unexpected, like holiday favorites and pop songs. Popular performances include events where movies like *The Nightmare Before Christmas* and *Star Wars: A New Hope* play on the Orpheum's large movie screen with original vocals and sound effects while the orchestra provides a live musical score! The Sioux City Symphony Orchestra also conducts community outreach and education, including the always popular "instrument petting zoo."

(712) 277-2111
SiouxCitySymphony.org

OBSERVE OPULENCE
AT THE ORPHEUM THEATRE

When the Sioux City Orpheum opened in 1927 as part of the famous Orpheum Circuit, it was the largest theater in the state of Iowa—an opulent architectural love letter to the fine arts, complete with a Wurlitzer organ. But as the entertainment industry changed, so did the fortunes of the Orpheum, and by the 1980s, it had been reduced to a rundown movie theater.

The Sioux City Orpheum returned to life in 2001 after a multi-million-dollar restoration, reopening as Sioux City's premiere venue for live entertainment and listed on the National Register of Historic Places. Today, the Orpheum hosts all kinds of high-caliber acts, from large-scale productions like full-length Broadway musicals, to elaborate magic shows, to pared-down performances from nationally renowned comedians and singers using nothing but a mic and a stool.

528 Pierce St.
(712) 244-5000 (box office)
OrpheumLive.com

ROCK AND ROLL
WITH THE ROCKESTRA

America's first professional rock orchestra, Sioux City's Rockestra, is a high-adrenaline fusion of two wonderful genres. Starring 40 professional musicians from throughout Siouxland, regularly joined by impressive guest stars, Rockestra always delivers rhythm, soul, and energy with an orchestral flavor that can't help but make you smile. Under the musical direction of founder John Luebke, Rockestra's amazing musicians use their vocal and instrumental skills to perform the biggest hits of rock and roll. In this unconventional orchestra, the classics mean Queen and Slash, and modern pieces mean Regina Spektor and Parachute. Sioux City Rockestra performs at the Orpheum, the Marquee, and other venues across Siouxland and around the world. And you can take the sounds of Rockestra home with you, too—Rockestra has an album available as a CD or digital download!

SiouxCityRockestra.com

ENJOY THE CLASSICS
AT THE LE MARS COMMUNITY THEATRE

With its roots in an evening drama class for adults in the 1960s, the Le Mars Community Theatre now has more than 50 years of experience bringing the magic of theater to the people of Siouxland. In its early days, the troupe performed in venues as diverse as nightclubs and the county courthouse. But since 1977, the Le Mars Community Theatre has occupied the 1914 post office building, now christened the Postal Playhouse. The Le Mars Community Theatre produces about four shows each year, with a particular focus on stage classics: musicals like *Little Shop of Horrors* and *The Music Man*, comedies like *Arsenic and Old Lace*, and more serious works like *Our Town* and *Of Mice and Men*. The Le Mars Community Theater has also performed two world premieres: *Letter to the Emperor* by Eleanor Phelps and *Gateway or Le Mars Is Born* by Betty Lou and Art Larson.

105 First St. NE
Le Mars, IA 51031
(712) 546-5788
LeMarsCommTheatre.org

SING ALONG
WITH THE SIOUX CITY MUNICIPAL BAND

For over a century, amateur musicians from around Siouxland have joined together in the Sioux City Municipal Band to bring the gift of big-band music to all. The band's weekly summer concerts are some of the most accessible music events in Siouxland. Every Sunday evening in the summertime, the Sioux City Municipal Band performs at the concrete, Art Deco bandshell in Sioux City's Grandview Park while the audience watches from the surrounding natural amphitheater. The shows are of the laid-back, come-as-you-are variety. Listeners sit on park benches or picnic blankets, children and puppies romp in the grass, and teens play on the disc golf course within earshot. The Sioux City Fire Department often holds an "open firetruck" for kids in the parking lot at the same time. The shows typically feature the tunes of famous big-band composers, but don't exclude classical, rock, pop, and movie soundtrack staples. And at every concert, the audience is encouraged to sing along!

Grandview Park
Facebook.com/SiouxCityMunicipalBand

CHEER FOR YOUR FAVORITES
AT THE TYSON EVENTS CENTER

Join up to 10,000 of your friends and neighbors at Sioux City's Tyson Events Center to catch all the fun a performance arena can bring! Built in 2002, immediately adjacent to the Municipal Auditorium, the Tyson is home to events for all ages. With convertible flooring, it transforms into a basketball court for the NAIA Women's Basketball Championship Tournament, an arena football field for the Sioux City Bandits, a dirt track for monster trucks, an ice rink for the Sioux City Musketeers, and an elaborate stage for everything from children's performers to an annual circus to classic rock and country musicians. As Sioux City's largest venue, whether the Tyson is hosting the Harlem Globetrotters, *Paw Patrol Live!*, or the Doobie Brothers, you won't want to miss the show.

401 Gordon Dr.
(712) 279-4850
TysonCenter.com

PUT ON A SHOW
WITH THE SIOUX CITY COMMUNITY THEATRE

The Sioux City Community Theatre (SCCT) is a non-professional performing arts organization that welcomes performers from throughout Siouxland to be part of the show! The productions at SCCT include children's shows, classic musicals, thoughtful modern pieces, adult comedies, and even dinner theater. Formed in 1948 with a $400 loan from the Sioux City Recreation Department, the SCCT performs at the old Shore Acres Ballroom near Riverside Park, which in its prior life had hosted the likes of Lawrence Welk, the Everly Brothers, and Frankie Avalon. Now with over 70 seasons under its dramatic belt, the SCCT continues to grow and innovate, proving time and time again that many Siouxlanders are performers worth watching.

1401 Riverside Blvd.
(712) 233-2719
SCCTheatre.org

TIP
Billy Boy is just a mile north of the SCCT, so stop by for a milkshake after a show!

32

SEE THE CITY
FROM GRANDVIEW PARK

What do a Victorian rose garden, an Art Deco bandshell, contemporary street art, and disc golf all have in common? They're all part of what makes Grandview Park so special!

Grandview Park, Sioux City's largest city park, is the home of a spectacular white bandshell, a concrete stage in Art Deco style built as a public works project during the Great Depression. It hosts summer concerts, music festivals, and movies, but when not in official use, is open to the public to climb, sing, and dance on. Behind the bandshell is the Grandview Park Rose Garden. A popular venue for weddings, the rose garden features a large fountain, walking paths, and rows and rows of roses. Visitors will also find a playground, basketball courts, sledding hill, twin water towers covered with vibrant street art, a nine-hole disc golf course, and a view of all of Sioux City—which is grand indeed.

24th St. & Grandview Blvd.

TIP

Grandview Park is home to Siouxland's biggest Easter egg hunt. And on the Saturday closest to the Fourth of July, Grandview Park hosts Siouxland's biggest music festival—Saturday in the Park—which has included some of the biggest names in modern music, from Aretha Franklin to Kacey Musgraves, plus Siouxland's best fireworks show, and at least 20,000 other festivalgoers!

APPLAUD
THE LEWIS & CLARK THEATRE COMPANY

The Lewis & Clark Theatre Company, based in Yankton, South Dakota, is a performing arts troupe that has been producing shows for over 50 years. Their repertoire includes improv, theater classics, family-friendly shows for kids, and holiday favorites. LCTC, as the troupe is known, owns, operates, and performs in the Dakota Theatre, built as an opera house in 1902. Today, the Dakota Theatre is also used as a local music performance venue and a movie theater. LCTC is also known for its community benefit events, such as annual screenings of classic films where the price of admission is simply a canned good for the local food bank.

328 Walnut St.
Yankton, SD 57078
(605) 665-4711
LewisAndClarkTheatre.org

34

GET A SONG STUCK IN YOUR HEAD
AT THE NATIONAL MUSIC MUSEUM

Forget "Seventy-Six Trombones"! The National Music Museum, on the University of South Dakota campus in Vermillion, has more than 200! They're part of the museum's amazing collection of over 15,000 musical instruments, including the oldest cello known to exist and a guitar played by Elvis Presley. The museum opened in 1973, and the *New York Times* has lauded it as a "musical Smithsonian." The National Music Museum closed for a couple of years for an extensive multiyear renovation, but is set to open even better than before in 2021, with a new 16,000-square-foot expansion. In addition to housing more of its collection, the new space will include areas dedicated to live performances, education, and instrument preservation.

414 E Clark St.
Vermillion, SD 57069
(605) 658-3450
NMMUSD.org

PRAISE WITH THE BROWNS

Contemporary Christian and Southern gospel music fans won't want to miss the Browns. This band, members of a Le Mars farm family, performs at their own Browns Century Theater—that is, when the Browns aren't on tour and performing in places from Branson, Missouri, to Carnival cruises to churches across the nation. The Browns Century Theater was once the American Trust and Savings Bank, but after refitting serves as an event space and an intimate concert venue for the Browns and other occasional performers. The Browns are siblings Michaela, Adam, and Andrew, who began performing with their mother, Shelly, in the early 2000s. Now the three siblings, with their smooth harmonic vocals and Michaela's spectacular violin solos, have taken their music to the next level, creating a style best described as contemporary Southern gospel with a country edge. The Browns may just be the best-kept secret in contemporary Christian music, right here in Siouxland!

11 Central Ave. NW
Le Mars, IA 50131
(712) 546-5770
TheBrownsTheater.com
TheBrownsMusic.com

SING ALONG
WITH MUSICALS FROM THE NEW STAGE PLAYERS

They may be South Sioux City, Nebraska's only community theater and Siouxland's newest, but they're already making a big splash—the New Stage Players won the 2020 Siouxland Choice Awards for best local theater! New Stage Players productions include a variety of genres, and they're best known for entertaining children's musicals like *Frozen JR*. New Stage also serves as the local chapter of the Penguin Project, a national organization that partners with local theaters to help kids with special needs team up with other kids to put on full-scale musicals. Locally, this program has been a great success, bringing joy to the performers and audience alike with the inaugural production—*Annie Jr.*—in 2019.

3201 Dakota Ave.
South Sioux City, NE 68776
NewStagePlayers.com

COME YE
TO THE (WOODBURY COUNTY) FAIR

Blue-ribbon fun awaits at the Woodbury County Fairgrounds in Moville, Iowa! Spend a day—or several—at the Woodbury County Fair, and you'll find live music, homemade quilts, sack races, and pies baked with secret recipes, as well as the very best livestock and produce from Siouxland's farmers! Old Town at the fairgrounds is a special treat, featuring a small town's worth of buildings, all originally constructed in Woodbury County around the turn of the last century and now lovingly restored and moved to the fairgrounds. In Old Town, you can visit a one-room schoolhouse, a church, a general store, a train station, and a jail, all open to the public during the county fair each summer and used for community events and festivals throughout the year (like the Old Town Fall Fest and the Midwest Hot Rod Rally).

206 Fair St.
Moville, IA 51039
(833) 671-4493
WoodburyCountyFair.com

OTHER NOTABLE SIOUXLAND FAIRS

Clay County Fair
A big fair with big-name acts that calls itself
the "World's Greatest County Fair,"
and many locals agree

800 W 18th St.
Spencer, IA 51301
(712) 580-3000
ClayCountyFair.com

Plymouth County Fair
A midsized county fair full of
quintessential rural fun, billed as
"the best 5 days of summer"

500 Fourth Ave. NE
Le Mars, IA 51031
(712) 546-7835
PlymouthCountyFair.org

Dakota/Thurston Fair
A multicounty fair with a mix of traditions, like Jaripeo-style bull riding, reflecting both Nebraska's pioneer past and the local Hispanic population

1547 Stable Dr.
South Sioux City, NE 68733
(402) 610-0689
DakotaThurstonFairOnline.com

SPORTS AND RECREATION

STROLL
ALONG AMERICA'S LONGEST RIVER

Sioux City sits at the navigational headwaters of the mighty Missouri, the longest river in the United States. For decades, riverboats plied the river, transporting goods and passengers from Sioux City to the river's mouth, where it flows into the Mississippi at St. Louis. Today the passenger boats are mostly gone, but towboats still move barges of grain, marinas provide ample access for recreational watercraft, and the Missouri still offers an impressive view to those who stroll along its banks.

The riverfront in Sioux City has playgrounds, trails for walking or biking, and the Veterans Memorial Bridge spanning the Missouri River between Iowa and Nebraska, open to motor vehicles and pedestrians. The riverfront park's trails meander along the Missouri past a variety of attractions, from playgrounds, boat access, and scenic views, to the Anderson Dance Pavilion, Lewis & Clark Interpretive Center and Betty Strong Encounter Center, Flight 232 Memorial, the Sgt. Floyd Welcome Center, a historic US Route 20 commemorative marker, and even a hotel and restaurant. The Missouri is the must-see heart of Siouxland.

START YOUR ENGINE
AT PARK JEFFERSON INTERNATIONAL SPEEDWAY

If you feel the need for speed, along with precision driving, fresh air, lots of dirt, and plenty of quirky cars, Siouxland has you covered.

In the 1980s, local businessman Ted Carlson brought the joy of car racing to Siouxland by founding Park Jefferson just a few miles north of Sioux City in Jefferson, South Dakota. And today you can live out your racing-fan dreams at Park Jefferson International Speedway, where the three-eighths-of-a-mile dirt track features weekly races during spring, summer, and fall. Come hear the roar of six classes of International Motor Contest Association race cars, from championship spring cars to super-late models and much more!

48426 332nd St.
North Sioux City, SD 57049
(712) 202-5540
ParkJeff.com

MAKE A SPLASH
AT SIOUXLAND POOLS

As the mercury rises, get ready to dive deep (or just dip your toe) into some of Siouxland's best places to splash and swim. Sioux City's premier public pool is at Riverside Park, where swimmers enjoy twin water slides, a zero-depth entry, dump buckets, and other fun features. The Norm Waitt Sr. YMCA in South Sioux City, Nebraska, offers one of Siouxland's best indoor pools and a great view of the Missouri River. More than a half-dozen free public splash pads dot parks throughout Sioux City, with two of them at the south end of Riverside Park in the Miracle Field accessible sports complex. Check out the All Seasons Center in Sioux Center, Iowa, where visitors can ice skate in winter, climb a 16-foot rock wall, and enjoy both a pool and splash pad indoors. The adjoining Siouxnami Waterpark is Siouxland's only waterpark and was chosen by the Iowa Tourism Awards as "Outstanding Attraction" of 2020.

Riverside Park
1301 Riverside Blvd., Sioux-City.org

Norm Waitt Sr. YMCA, 601 Riverview Dr.
South Sioux City, NE 68776
(402) 404-8439, NWSYMCA.org

Siouxnami Waterpark & All Seasons Center
770 Seventh St. NE, Sioux Center, IA 51250
(712) 722-4386, SiouxCenter.org/139/All-Seasons-Center

GLIDE DOWNHILL
AT CONE PARK

Honored as Iowa's best new destination in 2018, Cone Park is situated on a hill on the east side of Sioux City. In winter, Cone Park's snow machines keep its 700-foot tubing hill perfectly cultivated for everything from snow glow tubing to cardboard sled races. Visitors can also enjoy a skating rink, which doubles as a splash pad in warmer months, and then warm up in the cozy lodge or around the outdoor fire pit. A two-mile walking trail loop leads around the hill to Sertoma Park, which features a large playground, a picturesque pond, and a challenging disc golf course. At the top of the hill between the two parks stands an iconic water tower emblazoned with a tribute to the song "Sioux City Sue."

3800 Line Dr.
(712) 279-6126
ConeParkSiouxCity.com

THROW YOUR BEST
AT SIOUXLAND DISC GOLF COURSES

It's hard to beat disc golf for a laid-back, family-friendly way to get some exercise and have fun too. With dozens of disc golf courses throughout Siouxland, players will have no trouble finding a place to play. Found mostly in parks, but also on college and hospital campuses, Siouxland's disc golf courses offer something for everyone, from the 1,210-foot, nine-hole course at Grandview Park in Sioux City, which features easy hills and few obstructions and is great for beginners and kids, to the 7,300-foot, advanced-level 18-hole course at the Mental Health Institute campus in Cherokee, Iowa, with an 880-foot par five.

RECOMMENDED SIOUXLAND DISC GOLF COURSES

Grandview Park
Nine holes
24th St. & Grandview Blvd.

Mental Health Institute
18 holes
1251 W Cedar Loop
Cherokee, IA 51012

West Floyd Park
18 holes
1024 Third St. SW
Le Mars, IA 51031

Hillview Recreation Area
Nine holes
25601 C60
Hinton, IA 51024

Roadside Park
Nine holes
Highway 10 & Third St.
Alton, IA 51003

Crystal Cove
18 holes
W 39th St. & Timberline Dr.
South Sioux City, NE 68776

JUMP FOR JOY
AT DROPZONE

Jump, climb, game, and more at DropZone Family Fun Center, Siouxland's only trampoline park. Part of the park—called the Little Tykes Area—is exclusively for preschoolers and toddlers, so they can safely join in the bouncing. DropZone also features a "ninja"-style obstacle course, a laser tag arena, and an expansive arcade. Parents can hang out in the lounge and enjoy drinks, TV, and a golf simulator. When it's time to refuel, the snack bar offers pizza, tacos, burgers, and drinks. DropZone is one of Siouxland's best bets for birthday parties, or any party, with several private rooms available.

3840 Stadium Dr.
(712) 522-1722
DropZoneFFC.com

KAYAK TO YOUR CAMPSITE
AT DANISH ALPS

Danish Alps State Recreation Area, just outside Hubbard, Nebraska, consists of 520 acres of beautiful parkland and over 200 acres of sparkling Kramper Lake. The park opened in 2015, its name a tribute to the Danish American settlers who built their homesteads in the area in the 1800s. Today, visitors enjoy this peaceful park in all seasons. Spring and summer are perfect for no-wake boating on the lake, camping, birdwatching for eagles and pelicans, fishing from the ADA-accessible dock (for bluegill, bass, crappie, catfish, and walleye), hiking, and horseback riding on the trails! Six campsites are accessible only by water, delighting kayakers and canoers who want a secret getaway. In autumn, the park becomes a haven for hunters. And in winter, try cross-country skiing on the park's many trails!

1260 200th St.
Hubbard, NE 68741
(402) 632-4109
OutdoorNebraska.gov/DanishAlps

TAKE ME OUT
TO A SIOUX CITY EXPLORERS BALLGAME

Don some black, red, and white and enjoy America's pastime with the Sioux City Explorers at Lewis and Clark Park. The Explorers—known locally as the "X's"—are part of the American Association of Independent Professional Baseball, and they play against teams from throughout the central United States and Canada. The X's have won several division championships since their founding in 1993 and have twice been league runner-up, so expect fast, quality gameplay, affordable ticket prices, jersey giveaways, T-shirt cannons, and a good view from any seat in the house. The X's also pay tribute to Siouxland's history—their name hearkens back to Lewis and Clark's expedition to explore the Louisiana Purchase for President Thomas Jefferson, and their mascot Slider is a black Newfoundland like the pup who accompanied them on their journey. Batter up!

Mercy Field at Lewis and Clark Park
3400 Line Dr.
(712) 277-9467
XsBaseball.com

TIP
Sioux City Explorers games in early July are among Sioux City's best bets for fireworks!

SWING LOW
AT SIOUXLAND GOLF COURSES

From scratch golfers to old duffers, if you want to hit the links, Siouxland's many golf courses offer something for everyone. Among the best is the Dakota Dunes Country Club just across the Big Sioux River in South Dakota. Designed by Arnold Palmer, the Dakota Dunes course was a regular feature on the PGA Nationwide Tour in the 1990s and is consistently ranked as the best course in South Dakota. Many of the other local courses offer nine or 18 holes of challenging play with prairie and woodland views that are well worth the time of any golfer living in or visiting Siouxland. The Iowa Golf Association even chose the Meadows in Moville as their nine-hole Course of the Year in 2012 to honor its excellence. Need a golf experience that's a little smaller? North Forty is the place in Siouxland for a classic mini golf experience!

Dakota Dunes Country Club
960 S Dakota Dunes Blvd.
Dakota Dunes, SD 57049
(605) 232-3000
DakotaDunesCountryClub.com

North Forty
Miniature golf
3700 North US Highway 75
(712) 239-5909
NorthFortyMiniGolf.com

MORE SIOUXLAND GOLF COURSES

The Meadows Country Club
1483 Humboldt Ave.
Moville, IA
(712) 873-3184
MeadowsCountryClub.com

Whispering Creek Golf Club
6500 Whispering Creek Dr.
(712) 276-3678
WhisperingCreekGolfClub.com

Green Valley Golf Course
4300 Donner Ave.
(712) 252-2025
GreenValleyFloyd.com

Brookside Golf Club
101 Highway 140
Kingsley, IA 51028
(712) 378-2595

Anthon Golf Club
2238 Highway 31
Anthon, IA 51004
(712) 373-5774

Two Rivers Golf Club
150 S Oak Tree Ln.
Dakota Dunes, SD 57049
(605) 232-3241
GolfTwoRivers.com

REACH NEW HEIGHTS
AT THE LONG LINES FAMILY RECREATION CENTER

Looking for the best climbing wall between Chicago and Denver? Look no further! Long Lines Family Rec Center in Sioux City features a towering 50-foot rock wall, as well as several smaller walls and structures. Long Lines also offers indoor batting cages and courts for volleyball and basketball. One highlight for young families is the free "Tiny Tots open gym" on weekday mornings! The center also serves as a municipal arena for graduations, health fairs, and other community events. The Long Lines Family Rec Center was once Sioux City's municipal auditorium, and is attached to the Tyson Events Center.

401 Gordon Dr.
(712) 224-5124
Sioux-City.org

48

WATCH THE BEST
AT THE NAIA CHAMPIONSHIPS

In Siouxland, March means basketball. The Tyson Events Center has long hosted the National Association of Intercollegiate Athletics (NAIA) Division II women's basketball national championship tournament. In 2018, the NAIA made the decision to eliminate divisions in basketball beginning in 2020, and from now on, Sioux City's Tyson Events Center will host the new NAIA women's basketball national championship tournament! Teams from across the country—and from Sioux City's two four-year colleges, Morningside College and Briar Cliff University—compete in what is always a fast-paced and fun-to-watch series of games.

The Tyson Events Center also hosts the NAIA women's volleyball championship every fall!

NAIA.org

HIT THE ICE
AT SIOUXLAND SKATING RINKS

Glide across the ice—or let a hockey puck or curling stone do the gliding for you. At Sioux City's IBP Ice Center, visitors can enjoy the classic ice-skating experience as they sail along the Zamboni-smoothed surface. A party room is available for birthdays, and outside public skating times, the IBP hosts youth hockey, figure skating, and more. For more fun on ice, check out the Yankton Ice Rink in Yankton, South Dakota, which likewise offers open public skating and party-room rental. In deep winter, head to an outdoor ice rink in a local park—every year Sioux City's Leif Erickson Park and Yankton's Tripp and Sertoma Parks create free outdoor rinks for the enjoyment of all.

IBP Ice Center
3808 Stadium Dr.
(712) 279-4880
Sioux-City.org

MORE ICE RINKS

Leif Erickson Park
31st St. & Virginia St.
Sioux-City.org

Yankton Ice Rink
901 Whiting Dr.
Yankton, SD 57078
(605) 665-0229
YanktonIce.org

Tripp Park
Eighth & Broadway
Yankton, SD 57078
(605) 668-5234
CityofYankton.org

Sertoma Park
15th St. & Ferdig Ave.
Yankton, SD 57078
(605) 668-5234
CityofYankton.org

50

ENJOY INCLUSIVE PLAY
AT MIRACLE FIELD

Miracle Field is a big name to live up to, but the smiles on the faces of kids with and without special needs as they play side by side demonstrate that this unique part of Sioux City's Riverside Park is aptly named. Miracle Field's two splash pads, two adaptive playgrounds, musical sensory playground, accessible baseball field, and wheelchair-accessible mini golf course, all free, make it one of the Midwest's best inclusive play spaces, well worth a visit for any family with young children—or the young at heart!

The rest of Riverside Park is also worth any visitor's time, with Sioux City's best public pool and waterslide, two standard playgrounds, tons of green space, soccer fields, a great view of South Dakota across the Big Sioux River, and trails that run all the way to Chris Larsen Park near downtown.

1301 Riverside Blvd.
MiracleLeagueofSiouxCity.com

TIP

Miracle Field is just across from the Bruguier Cabin, also in Riverside Park, so it's easy to visit both in the same trip!

WHEEL AROUND AT ROLLERAMA

Strap on some skates and step back in time at Rollerama in Sioux City, where the roller rink party never stopped! Full of nostalgia for those who remember roller skating in the 1970s or the rollerblading craze of the 1990s, but just as fun for newbies, Rollerama offers a classic skating rink experience. Strap on your khaki-colored rental skates and glide along the perfectly smooth wooden floor while the DJ plays the latest tunes and all the classics, too. And be ready when it's time for the couples skate (when couples hold hands) or the hokeypokey! When you need a break, have a seat at a table in the snack bar. Rollerama is also a great place for birthday parties and fundraisers!

4500 Stone Ave.
(712) 276-9500
RolleramaOnline.com

52

GET A LOW SCORE
AT RUSH WERKS OR YANKTON BOWL

For Sioux City's best bowling experience, head to Rush Werks. There you'll find 12 classic bowling lanes, music, lights, an arcade, and high-tech screens. The food at Clyde's Grill & Pub, attached to the bowling alley, puts most bowling alley snack bars to shame! A local favorite is the steakhouse burger: prime rib, blue cheese crumbles, cabernet mushrooms, and haystack onions.

Or check out Yankton Bowl in Yankton, South Dakota, with 20 lanes, arcade games, a room for video-lottery gaming, and quintessential bowling alley food from pizza and beer to burgers. You can also try South Dakota's official state nosh: chislic—fried cubes of tender lamb!

3828 Stadium Dr.
(712) 252-4545
RushWerks.com

3010 Broadway Ave.
Yankton, SD 57078
(605) 665-7638
YanktonBowl.com

ADMIRE RIVERSIDE TRAILS AT ADAMS HOMESTEAD AND NATURE PRESERVE

On a South Dakota peninsula, between the Big Sioux River (and then Iowa) on the east, and the Missouri River (and then Nebraska) on the west, you'll find a charming state park called Adams Homestead and Nature Preserve. The 1,500-acre park offers educational programming, special events throughout the year, and opportunities to enjoy nature with your family. Hiking and biking trails are available when it's warm, and in winter the trails are groomed for cross-country skiing. Park-goers can also practice their archery at an on-site range, play at an adorable playground, and visit Sonny's farm, a working farm with animals kids can study and pet. Several buildings at the park date back to the late 1800s, when Stephen Searls Adams built the homestead after which the park is named.

272 Westshore Dr.
McCook Lake, SD 57049
(605) 232-0873
gfp.sd.gov/parks/detail/Adams-Homestead-And-Nature-Preserve

54

GET SPACEY
AT THE FRED G. DALE PLANETARIUM

Reach for the stars at Wayne State College's Fred G. Dale Planetarium in Wayne, Nebraska! The planetarium offers an unforgettable immersive experience, and with 3 million pixels projected on its dome, it can show up to 500 million stars at a time. College students and visiting field trips use the dome for academic lectures, but it shines most with movies on a wide variety of topics, from preschool-level astronomy basics with beloved television characters to college-level discussions of dark matter. The planetarium also has VR goggles, which the public can use to experience a variety of educational and entertaining programs. Outside the theater dome, a small collection of telescopes and astronomical models forms a mini-museum of astronomy. Presentations open to the public are held regularly, and one weekend each month is dedicated to planetarium shows for kids.

Carhart Science Building
1111 Main St.
Wayne, NE 68787
(402) 375-7471
WSC.edu/info/20091/planetarium

TOSS THE PIGSKIN
WITH STAMPEDE AND BANDITS FOOTBALL

Sioux City has two great choices for football! Don your black and yellow and get ready to cheer on the Sioux City Stampede, Sioux City's amateur football team! The Stampede play at Memorial Field in Sioux City, and they play well. In their two years participating in the Northern Elite Football League, the Stampede made it to the championship twice and won once!

Or try black and red for the Sioux City Bandits, the local arena football team. The Bandits currently compete in the Champions Indoor Football league, and play their home games at the Tyson Events Center. For fast-paced, up-close action—forward motion, tackles into the arena wall, and footballs flying into the stands!—nothing beats arena football. And the Bandits deliver: since their formation in 1999, they have made the playoffs 13 times, and have won three league championships!

Facebook.com/SiouxCityStampede
SCBandits.com

TIP

Sioux Falls, South Dakota, a city about an hour north, has a hockey team also called Stampede, so check game info carefully to be sure which Stampede is playing!

HIKE MORE LOESS
AT STONE STATE PARK

Nestled in the northwest corner of Sioux City, you'll find Stone State Park, over 1,000 acres of woodland and prairie hills at the northernmost point of Iowa's geologically unique Loess Hills. Stone State Park features eight miles of hiking, equestrian, and mountain-bike trails, all with plenty of elevation change and opportunity to observe local wildlife. The park also offers a fishing pond, picnic shelters, grills, and picnic tables. During the Great Depression, the Civilian Conservation Corps built stone bridges, tunnels, entrance markers, and a lodge in the park, all of which are still in use. The lodge, available for rent, is a charming event venue. For those who wish to stay the night, camping cabins, as well as sites for tents and RVs, are available.

5001 Talbot Rd.
(712) 255-4698
IowaDNR.gov

BURROW LIKE A BADGER
AT THE DOROTHY PECAUT NATURE CENTER

If you want to make s'mores, go for a snowshoe hike, learn about loess soil, or touch a turtle, the Dorothy Pecaut Nature Center in Sioux City is the place to go. Inside the nature center you'll find exhibits about the geology, flora, and fauna of Siouxland, including live rescued animals, preserved animal artifacts, and hands-on learning stations for kids. The short, carefully manicured trails outside the nature center offer people of all ages a chance to explore Siouxland's natural wonders, and the nature playground just up the trails is indisputably one of Siouxland's best. On the backside of the building is a raptor house, home to several rescued birds including an owl and a hawk. The nature center produces some of the best educational events around, from monthly preschool story times to summer camps for schoolkids, to wilderness and camping skills classes for teens and adults.

4500 Sioux River Rd.
(712) 258-0838
WoodburyParks.org/Dorothy-Pecaut-Nature-Center/

GEAR UP FOR REV-TAC

If you're interested in shooting sports or self-defense, Rev-Tac in Jackson, Nebraska, is the closest thing to paradise you'll find in this world. A monthly membership buys you and your family access to a pistol range and a rifle range. But Rev-Tac is much, much more than just a typical shooting range. On the range, you can punch paper or ping steel, and you can even train with provided obstacles like barricades and old vehicles. And Rev-Tac's staff—many of whom are current or former military or law enforcement, and all of whom are both informative and entertaining—offer all the training opportunities you can imagine and then some: classes to qualify for concealed-carry permits, monthlong practical pistol courses, basic and advanced rifle programs, pistol test-drives (try before you buy!) and, of course, basic emergency trauma management (mandatory for all range members). Most classes are open to non-members, with discounts for members.

1545 Knox Blvd.
Jackson, NE 68743
(712) 253-8810
Rev-Tac.com

GO BIRDWATCHING
AT PONCA STATE PARK

At Ponca State Park in Ponca, Nebraska, you can wake to the sun rising over the Missouri River just outside your tent or cabin and then spend your day kayaking, fishing, riding on a guided horseback tour, and resting under the shade of a 350-year-old oak tree on the banks of the Mighty Mo. Another highlight for visitors is the opportunity to throw the atlatl, an ancient weapon used by the people indigenous to this area, at the Eric Wiebe Shooting Complex. Ponca State Park is home to seasonal events like the Missouri River Outdoor Expo every summer, Hallowfest in fall, and Winterfest and a Fruitcake Fling every winter. The park includes 22 miles of hiking trails, an indoor nature center, and a new aquatic center.

88090 Spur 26 E.
Ponca, NE 68770
(402) 755-2284
OutdoorNebraska.gov/Ponca

60

CHECK (OUT)
THE SIOUX CITY MUSKETEERS

Don your green and gold and head to the Tyson Events Center to cheer on the Sioux City Musketeers! The Musketeers have been representing Sioux City in the United States Hockey League, a Tier I junior league, since the 1972–73 season. Since that time, the Muskies (as locals call them) have sent more than two dozen players to the NHL and made it to the playoffs more than three dozen times, and the Muskies won the USHL's Clark Cup three times: in 1982, 1986, and 2002! The Sioux City Musketeers are absolutely beloved by the people of Sioux City, and with good reason—you won't find a better sports experience in Siouxland than a Muskies game!

MusketeersHockey.com

FISH AND RELAX
AT SOUTHWOOD CONSERVATION AREA

The Southwood Conservation Area in Smithland, Iowa, is a scenic forested retreat with lots to do. Stay in a rustic cabin, where you can watch a movie on the cabin's Blu-ray player or native birds through the window—bluebird boxes are posted throughout the park. The ponds at Southwood offer excellent fishing for stocked bluegill, catfish, and bass, and boats are restricted to electric trolling motors. Use a self-guided nature walk brochure, available at the trailheads, to try to spot whitetail deer and turkeys, and to view plots of native grasses. In the wintertime, you can enjoy ice fishing and cross-country skiing. Game wardens permit limited hunting—no centerfire rifles—from October 15 to May 15, away from developed areas. Regardless of the time of year, for fun in Siouxland's great outdoors, Southwood Conservation Area can't be beat!

3402 330th St.
Smithland, IA 51056
(712) 899-2215
WoodburyParks.org/Southwood-Conservation-Area

SAY YES TO SALIX

The tiny town of Salix, Iowa, just a few minutes south of Sioux City, was founded in the mid-1800s by several families of French-Canadian immigrants, who named it after the willow trees that lined the riverbanks ("salix" is the Latin word for "willow"). Today, Salix is home to two small lakes formed by old Missouri River oxbows: 600-acre Brown's Lake, surrounded by Bigelow Park, and Snyder Bend with its adjacent park. Both parks feature a public beach, campsites, cabins, and picnic shelters. Boaters and water skiers can access the lakes using available boat ramps. And at both Brown's Lake and Snyder Bend, the fishing is great! Try your hand at catching walleye, largemouth bass, northern pike, bluegill, crappie, catfish, and perch.

722 Bigelow Park Rd.
Salix, IA 51052
(712) 946-7114
WoodburyParks.org/Browns-Lake-Bigelow-Park

2924 Snyder Bend Rd.
Salix, IA 51052
(712) 946-5622

DRIVE THE LOESS HILLS SCENIC BYWAY

The Loess Hills are Siouxland's most unique geological feature. They consist of 100-foot bluffs of windblown glacial silt. The silt, called loess (pronounced "luss"), was formed when glaciers pulverized boulders into powder during the last ice age. Hills made of such extensive deposits of loess exist in exactly two places in the world: western Iowa and a remote corner of China! One of the best ways to experience the Loess Hills is by driving the Loess Hills Scenic Byway, which runs about 200 miles from just north of Sioux City to the Missouri border in southwest Iowa. Get ready for winding roads through deciduous forest, seas of prairie grass, and cute little towns dotting the way. You can also explore the Loess Hills on foot, hiking, camping, or hunting at Five Ridge Prairie State Preserve in rural Plymouth County.

Loess Hills Scenic Byway
VisitLoessHills.org

Five Ridge Prairie Preserve
15561 260th St.
Westfield, IA 51062

SEE WHAT'S FISHY
AT GAVINS POINT

Gavins Point Dam straddles the border of Nebraska and South Dakota, spanning 1.9 miles across the Missouri River, as the Mighty Mo's furthest downstream dam. Despite its name, it's not actually built on the bluff called Gavins Point; although originally planned for that hill, the dam project was eventually moved to its current location, nearby Calumet Bluff. This bluff was where Lewis and Clark's 1804 expedition first met leaders of the Sioux people (they called the bluff White Bear Cliff). The dam's reservoir is a 31,000-acre lake named for those two explorers, offering all the fishing and recreation fun one might expect on a lake of that size. The surrounding Lewis and Clark Recreation Area, one of South Dakota's most popular, features playgrounds, beaches, marinas, three campgrounds, equestrian trails, a resort and restaurant, and even an archery range! Visitors can also hike along the river or check out the visitor center and gift shop. During summer, tour the hydroelectric power plant at the dam or view more than 10,000 gallons of display aquarium tanks at the Gavins Point National Fish Hatchery & Aquarium.

Lewis and Clark Visitor Center
55245 Highway 121, Crofton, NE 68730, (402) 667-2546
GFP.sd.gov/parks/detail/Lewis-and-Clark-Recreation-Area

Gavins Point National Fish Hatchery & Aquarium
31227 436th Ave., Yankton, SD 57078, (605) 665-3352
FWS.gov/mountain-prairie/fisheries/GavinsPoint.php

TIP

Plan a visit to the Lewis and Clark Recreation Area in January to see bald eagles, as many of the majestic birds make their homes in the trees lining the banks of the Missouri River!

CULTURE AND HISTORY

65

PAY TRIBUTE
TO CHIEF WAR EAGLE

The story of Siouxland is, in part, the story of the confluence of the Missouri and Big Sioux Rivers, and the story of the people who came to live in the surrounding river basins in Iowa, Nebraska, and South Dakota. So, it's fitting to begin any journey into the area's history by visiting War Eagle Park and the War Eagle Monument. High on a bluff, where visitors can look out over the meeting of two rivers and three states, stands a statue of Yankton Sioux Chief War Eagle. There's also a smaller monument to Theophile Bruguier, a fur trader who was Sioux City's first white settler and eventually became War Eagle's son-in-law. Visitors to War Eagle Park should also check out the old Missouri River Trail marker close to the park's entrance—this rock marking an old fur trapper trail was lost for decades, and only recently found and restored!

4000 War Eagle Dr.

BUZZ BY
BRUGUIER CABIN

When it's open on one Sunday every month during the summer, visitors can take a peek into Bruguier Cabin, home to Sioux City's first white settler. Theophile Bruguier was a fur trader who came to Siouxland from Canada in the 1840s. He is most famous for his friendship with Chief War Eagle of the Yankton Sioux, and for marrying two of Chief War Eagle's daughters, Flaming Cloud and Dawn. Inside the cabin at Riverside Park, visitors will find a mini-museum of pioneer artifacts and a beautiful stone fireplace, all of which offer a glimpse into what frontier life was like for Bruguier and the other pioneers who put down their roots in Siouxland in the middle of the 19th century.

1301 Riverside Blvd.

67

SEE THE SAFE
IN CALLIOPE VILLAGE

Historic Calliope Village in present-day Hawarden, Iowa, offers a glimpse into life in early Siouxland and also preserves a memory of a fascinating long-ago conflict. In the late 1800s, as the first pioneers settled in Sioux County, the town of Calliope was designated the county seat. However, as neighboring Orange City grew in population and cultural prominence, a fierce rivalry arose between the towns, with the Orange City residents vying to seize the county seat mantle. Eventually, the safe holding the county government records was stolen from the courthouse in Calliope and moved to Orange City, and with it went the status of county seat! Today, Orange City remains the county seat of Sioux County, but the old safe is back in Calliope, and you can visit it in Calliope Village's reproduction of Sioux County's first courthouse. Calliope Village features a variety of other historical Sioux County buildings, some reproduced, but many authentic from the 1800s and early 1900s. Calliope Village is also home to community events, including a festival each summer.

IA 10 & 19th St.
Hawarden, IA 51023

CRUISE AMERICA'S LONGEST ROADWAY

Historic US Highway 20, running through Sioux City and much of Siouxland, is the longest road in the United States. Running from Boston, Massachusetts, to Newport, Oregon, Highway 20's heyday was before the dawn of the interstate system, when traveling meant seeing the sights in each cute little town along the way. You can relive those days today by heading to Jackson, Nebraska, where you'll find the oldest malt shop on Highway 20: Andy's Sweet Tooth Drive Inn. This family-owned eatery continues to delight visitors with malts, burgers, and other classic drive-in fare. The chocolate malts are the most iconic, but look for specialty flavors like the Bing mixer—inspired by Palmer Candy Company's Twin Bing!

While you're in Jackson, head a bit further west along Highway 20 to find the Sentinels of the Prairie, a collection of almost two dozen vintage windmills dating from the 1880s through the 1930s. Most of the windmills came from Nebraska farms, where they helped pull water out of wells, but some came from farther-away places like Texas. All the windmills offer a fascinating look into the history of this part of the country.

Sentinels of the Prairie, Jackson, NE

Andy's Sweet Tooth Drive Inn
123 W Elk St., Jackson, NE 68743
(402) 632-4245

TWIRL AROUND WINDMILL PARK
AND THE ORANGE CITY TULIP FESTIVAL

At the heart of Orange City, Iowa, you'll find Windmill Park. The park pays homage to the city's heritage with reproduction Dutch windmills, like a 13th century-style molen, and also features a modern playground as well as a castle-inspired bandshell that gives every show a bit of Dutch flair. Windmill Park is home to family-friendly events all year, most notably in May when Orange City hosts one of the best tulip festivals in the world. Since 1936, the Orange City Tulip Festival has been celebrating Dutch heritage and springtime. Today, the festival includes parades led by traditional street washers, plus live wooden shoe carving demonstrations, a Dutch street organ, traditional dancing, horse-drawn trolley tours, a quilt show, puppet shows, and about 50,000 tulips—many of them planted in Windmill Park.

Orange City Tulip Festival
Held at venues throughout the city
OCTulipFestival.com

Windmill Park
206 Central Ave. NW
Orange City, IA 51041

DO THE CHICKEN DANCE
IN WAYNE

Welcome to Wayne, America! The Blue Cat Gallery in Wayne, Nebraska, is a hub of the fine arts for this community of 5,000, with art in a variety of media available for public viewing or purchase and art classes for kids. Blue Cat displays art from any interested artist who meets the gallery's standards, with a particular focus on Siouxland artists. The gallery also participates in one of the quirkiest festivals in America: the Wayne Chicken Show. This annual summer festival takes place in venues across the city of Wayne, with chicken-themed activities from chicken-calling contests (whose winners often end up on the late-night talk show circuit!) to chicken dancing, to chicken art—including a juried, rural-themed art exhibit at the Blue Cat Gallery.

Blue Cat Gallery
114 W Third St.
Wayne, NE 68787
BlueCatGalleryStudio.com

POP INTO A CUTE LITTLE MUSEUM

Fascinating local city and county museums pepper the Siouxland landscape. Many of these occupy homes that once belonged to a prominent resident, and most, staffed by volunteers, open only a few days per week or month, or even by appointment only. But these little museums are gems that offer the most authentic look into the history of the areas they represent, and are well worth a trip for any historically minded visitor. The Century Home in Orange City, for example, was home to Judge Oosterhout, who served as a judge on the United States Court of Appeals for the Eighth Circuit. The Wayne County Historical Museum occupies the shingle-style mansion named after Rollie Ley, the bank president who once resided there. And the Union County Museum in Elk Point, South Dakota, is in the former home of pioneer Charles Murtha. For a slight change of pace, the Plymouth County Museum in Le Mars, Iowa, is an old school and the Angel De Cora Museum is on the campus of Little Priest Tribal College. In Sergeant Bluff, Iowa, a downtown storefront holds the Sergeant Bluff Museum's treasure trove of artifacts.

SIOUXLAND MUSEUMS OF LOCAL HISTORY

Angel De Cora Museum and Research Center
610 E College Dr.
Winnebago, NE 68071
(402) 257-5587
WinnebagoTribe.com

Century Home
318 Albany Ave. NE
Orange City, IA 51041
(712) 707-4510
DutchHeritageBoosters.com/History-2

Wayne County Historical Museum
(402) 375-1278
CityOfWayne.org/453/Wayne-County-Museum

Plymouth County Museum
335 First Ave. SW
Le Mars, IA 51031
(712) 546-7002
PlymouthCountyMuseum.webstarts.com

Sergeant Bluff Historical Museum
409 Fourth St.
Sergeant Bluff, IA 51054
(712) 943-2028
SergeantBluffMuseum.com

Union County Historical Society
707 W Main St.
Elk Point, SD 57025
(605) 761-0247
ElkPoint.org/Union-County-Historical-Museum/

REMEMBER THE PAST
AT THE FLIGHT 232 MEMORIAL

At the Flight 232 Memorial in Chris Larsen Park along Sioux City's riverfront, visitors can celebrate heroism and mourn those who died from the crash of United Airlines flight 232. The memorial depicts National Guard Colonel Dennis Nielsen carrying a child to safety, memorializing the astounding rescue by Nielsen and so many others after the historic airliner crash. Because of the pilots' ingenuity and calm after the plane lost all its hydraulic flight controls, along with the heroism of Siouxland's first responders, 184 people survived what experts say should have been an unsurvivable crash.

The nearby Anderson Dance Pavilion, also in Chris Larsen Park, is one of Siouxland's most scenic outdoor event spaces, featuring striking white columns, exquisitely landscaped flowers, and a covered concrete veranda that can host a banquet or serve as a stage. When not in use for an event, the pavilion and its grassy grounds are great for playing, picnicking, or simply enjoying a lovely view of the Missouri River.

Larsen Park Rd.

NAVIGATE
TO THE SERGEANT FLOYD RIVER MUSEUM AND WELCOME CENTER

Sioux City is situated at the navigational head of the Missouri River, so it's no surprise that riverboats have played a big role in its history. The Sergeant Floyd River Museum and Welcome Center is a fascinating and instructive commemoration of that history. The museum is on the *M.V. Sergeant Floyd*, a decommissioned military river inspection boat now in perpetual dry dock at Sioux City's riverfront park. Inside the museum, on the boat's first two decks, you'll find a wide variety of exhibits showcasing the history of the Missouri River in Siouxland, from tiny scale models of elaborate riverboats to authentic riverboat equipment to a full-size dugout canoe. On the top deck, visitors can view the restored captain's quarters, radio room, and pilot's wheelhouse, operate the controls, and even ring the boat's bell!

2000 Larsen Park Rd.
(712) 279-0198
SiouxCityMuseum.org/Sgt-Floyd-River-Museum-a-Welcome-Center

GAZE UPON THE SERGEANT FLOYD MONUMENT

The Lewis and Clark Expedition—also called the Corps of Discovery—traveled from the Illinois side of the Mississippi River up the Missouri. The journey continued over the Rockies, to the Pacific, and back, between May 1804 and September 1806, to explore the newly acquired Louisiana Purchase for President Thomas Jefferson. During that journey, the expedition suffered only one casualty: Sergeant Charles Floyd, who died on August 20, 1804, on a bluff in what is now Sioux City, Iowa. Floyd's grave is today marked by the Sergeant Floyd Monument—a 100-foot white sandstone obelisk erected atop a 100-foot loess bluff. The Department of the Interior later designated the 1901 monument as the first National Historic Landmark. The monument site features plaques, benches, sidewalks, and a spectacular view of the Missouri River. And a reenactment of Sergeant Floyd's burial is performed every August on the Saturday nearest to the anniversary of his death.

2601 S Lewis Blvd.

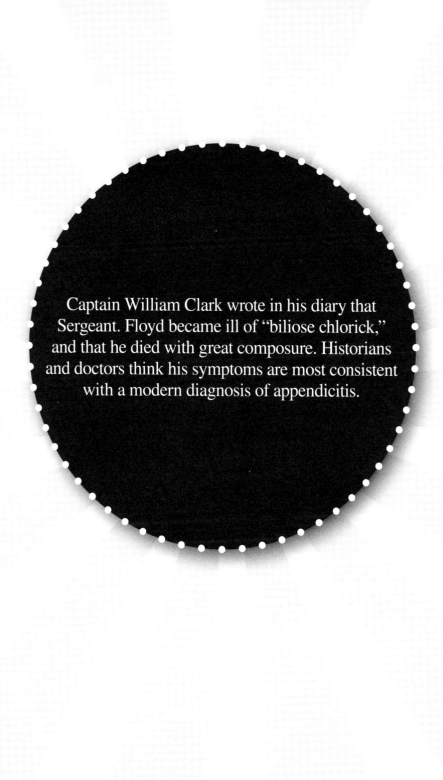

Captain William Clark wrote in his diary that Sergeant. Floyd became ill of "biliose chlorick," and that he died with great composure. Historians and doctors think his symptoms are most consistent with a modern diagnosis of appendicitis.

PLAY ALL DAY
AT LAUNCHPAD CHILDREN'S MUSEUM

LaunchPad Children's Museum is an interactive space where kids can stretch their legs and their brains. Much of LaunchPad pays a hands-on tribute to Siouxland's agricultural heritage. Kids can activate a plastic pellet grain elevator and climb through a big red barn. Future farmers can take toy vegetables from the field area to the mini-market to the play restaurant, serving their friends a tiny farm-to-table experience! Children blast off in a two-story playhouse shaped like a spaceship, experiment with scarves and balls in the wall of Bernoulli blowers, create their own structures in the Build Zone, and splash and play in an oversized water table. Families love the engaging educational programming at LaunchPad, from story times and STEM learning to summer camps and free events for kids with special needs.

623 Pearl St.
(712) 224-2542
LaunchPadMuseum.com

TAKE AN EXPEDITION
TO THE LEWIS AND CLARK INTERPRETIVE CENTER

Sioux City has the unique infamy of being the burial site of Sergeant Charles Floyd, the only person to die during the harrowing journey of the Corps of Discovery under Captain Meriwether Lewis and Lieutenant William Clark. At this interpretive center in Sioux City, visitors explore the famous expedition and its inextricable link to Siouxland. Animatronic versions of Lewis, Clark, Lewis's dog Seaman, President Thomas Jefferson, and Sergeant Floyd are some of the best permanent displays. While the interpretive center highlights the history of the expedition and in particular Sergeant Floyd, the attached Betty Strong Encounter Center focuses on the history and modern culture of the Native Americans in the region. The interpretive center also hosts unique musical and historical presentations, often before standing-room-only crowds.

900 Larsen Park Rd.
(712) 224-5242
SiouxCityLCIC.org

SOAR
AT THE MID AMERICA MUSEUM OF AVIATION & TRANSPORTATION

At Sioux City's Mid America Museum of Aviation & Transportation, visitors find an immersive lesson on transportation history from the roads to the skies. The museum's displays document transportation generally, but especially aviation, with all kinds of fascinating memorabilia, vehicles, and aircraft—both military and commercial! Especially noteworthy is the museum's moving tribute to United Flight 232, which crash-landed en route from Denver to Chicago at Sioux Gateway Airport in 1989 after an engine failure disrupted hydraulic flight controls. While the crash is the fifth deadliest in American aviation history, the flight crew, local first responders, medical professionals, and volunteers saved 184 lives, a laudable example of rescue done right.

2600 Expedition Ct.
(712) 252-5300
MidAmericaAirMuseum.org

> **TIP**
> The Flight 232 Memorial along the riverfront and the Flight 232 exhibit at the Sioux City Public Museum provide more information about this historic event.

78

HONOR LAW AND ORDER
AT THE POLICE MUSEUM AND CITY HALL

The Sioux City Police Museum, on the second floor of the police department headquarters, honors the proud history of our local law enforcement officers. The museum displays fascinating police memorabilia from across Sioux City's history—from badges and patches to uniforms, cuffs, and batons—as well as artwork celebrating Siouxland's courageous first responders. Highlights include photos by legendary local photographer George Lindblade and a one-of-a-kind drawing of a Sioux City K-9 officer by Siouxland artist Chuck Raymond. The museum is also the home of the Wall of Fallen Heroes, commemorating local officers who lost their lives in the line of duty.

Also worth a visit, just across the street, is Sioux City's City Hall—you can't miss its clock tower! Today's building is almost identical to the original constructed in the late 1800s as a federal building and modeled after the Palazzo Vecchio in Florence, Italy. After it became structurally unsound, the city completely rebuilt City Hall in the mid-1990s, reusing the original stone and iconic clock tower but expanding from four stories to five and providing modern interior amenities.

Sioux City Police Museum, 601 Douglas St.
(712) 279-6411, SiouxCityPolice.com/Sioux-City-Police-Museum

Sioux City Hall, 405 Sixth St.
(712) 279-6109, Sioux-City.org

79

DON'T ENTER ANY RAFFLES
AT THE PEIRCE MANSION

Real estate developer, cable car financier, railroad speculator, and—eventually—swindler John Peirce built Sioux City's most notable home at the corner of Jackson and 29th Streets in 1890. Constructed in the Richardsonian Romanesque style with a beautiful South Dakota quartzite exterior and positively opulent inside, the home's subsequent history is just as interesting as its architecture. When Peirce lost his shirt in an 1890s financial panic, he supposedly held a raffle for the house to restore his fortune, but the raffle was fixed! The house was privately owned until the 1950s, and from 1961 to 2011, it served as the Sioux City Public Museum. Today, the Peirce Mansion hosts weddings, showers, meetings, and a wide variety of other functions. Several rooms have been elaborately restored with period furnishings from the late 1890s, and the mansion opens to the public several times each year, with the annual Christmas Open House a particular favorite of Siouxlanders.

2901 Jackson St.
(712) 279-6174
SiouxCityMuseum.org/Peirce-Mansion

TIP

A block east of the Peirce Mansion, on 29th Street between Jones and Jennings Streets, you'll find Sunken Garden Park. The huge, unusual rocks in the park—called "moon rocks" by the locals—are actually smelted remnants from the plant that powered Sioux City's electric cable cars, which ran up and down Jackson Street in the 1890s!

GO BACK IN TIME
AT THE SIOUX CITY PUBLIC MUSEUM

From plesiosaurs to popcorn, the Sioux City Public Museum offers the most in-depth look at Sioux City history, and plenty of interactive fun, too. The museum's permanent collection showcases the entirety of Sioux City's history. Learn about Siouxland millions of years ago with fossils from the Western Interior Seaway and by digging for replicas in "the Big Dig." Admire artifacts from Siouxland's original inhabitants, including elaborate beadwork and a full-sized reproduction tepee. Experience pioneer life in a replica log cabin and view vehicles and technology from the 19th and 20th centuries. Visitors can also enjoy traveling temporary exhibits presenting historical and scientific lessons from around the world. Or join in on one of the museum's many history education events for all ages: story times, craft events, a local history competition for fourth graders, and lectures and walking tours for adults.

607 Fourth St.
(712) 279-6174
SiouxCityMuseum.org

SEEK SERENITY
AT TRINITY HEIGHTS

If you're looking for peace and inspiration, you can't go wrong with Trinity Heights. On a bluff which once was home to its namesake, the now-demolished Trinity High School and College, Trinity Heights is home to 14 acres of religious art, statues, and shrines. The stars of Trinity Heights are two three-story stainless-steel statues depicting Jesus and his mother Mary as "the Sacred Heart of Jesus" and "the Immaculate Heart of Mary Queen of Peace." Both are the work of renowned artist Dale Lamphere. You also won't want to miss the life-size sculptures based on Leonardo Da Vinci's *The Last Supper*—carved entirely from pine lumber!—in the St. Joseph Center. Outside, stroll along perfectly manicured sidewalks to observe dozens of statues of saints and biblical figures, from Moses to St. Francis of Assisi. The grounds include an outdoor cathedral, plaques about people and events significant in the Catholic faith, and a reproduction of the famous Grotto at Lourdes.

2511 33rd St.
(712) 239-8670
TrinityHeights.com

BE A CONNOISSEUR
AT THE SIOUX CITY ART CENTER

The Sioux City Art Center is Siouxland's premiere art museum, with temporary and permanent exhibits featuring artists from around the globe and a special focus on local and regional artists. Of particular note is Iowa-born Grant Wood's massive *Corn Room* mural on the third floor, a masterpiece in Wood's Regionalist offshoot of the broader Modernist art movement. The mural once graced the walls of a historic Sioux City hotel. You can also attend fancy parties for exhibit openings, regular performances by string quartets and chamber musicians, and more. On a less formal note, a special highlight for kids is the Junior League Hands On! Gallery, where kids can play with color, light, shape, and texture.

The art center is also Siouxland's hub for arts education, with art classes across all media and for every age group. Every year, the center exhibits works by local students and curates contests for art and sculpture. You can also thank the Sioux City Art Center for the beautiful and quirky sculptures beautifying street corners throughout downtown.

225 Nebraska St.
(712) 279-6272
SiouxCityArtCenter.org

TIP

For even more fun with art, drop in over Labor Day weekend for the Sioux City Art Center's ArtSplash—Siouxland's premier arts festival! ArtSplash hosts artists and performers from across the Midwest to display their work and perform in a city park, while local nonprofits invite attendees to their booths for hands-on art activities!

RISE ABOVE IT ALL
IN THE SIOUX CITY SKYWALK SYSTEM

In the 1970s, Sioux City created a convenient new way to enjoy its downtown: a system of "skywalks." The skywalks are fully enclosed, climate-controlled, elevated walkways that connect most of the buildings in downtown Sioux City. By using the skywalks, downtown visitors can walk from building to building in ease and comfort, whether in the depths of winter or on a blazing summer day, all without having to watch for traffic! Today visitors can access the skywalk from more than 25 access points, and the system extends around two miles in gridwork fashion over a dozen blocks, making it one of the 15 most extensive such systems in the United States. The skywalks offer the perfect way to walk between the library, the museum, the Orpheum Theatre, shopping, hotels, restaurants, offices, and other downtown attractions, or just to get some exercise when the weather is less than ideal. Don't miss the murals and historical photos on the skywalk walls!

ACCESSIBLE FROM THE SIOUX CITY SKYWALK:

Sioux City Public Library (Wilbur Aalfs Branch)
529 Pierce St.
(712) 255-2933
SiouxCityLibrary.org

Sioux City Convention Center
801 Fourth St.
(712) 279-4800
SiouxCityConventionCenter.com

Sweetwater Cafe
600 Fourth St.
(712) 224-4225
SweetwaterCafe.net

Orpheum Theatre
528 Pierce St.
(712) 244-5000
OrpheumLive.com

MercyOne Hospital
801 Fifth St.
(712) 279-2010
MercyOne.org/Siouxland

Art SUX Gallery
600 Fourth St. #105
(605)223-1278
ArtSUXGallery.com

STAY IN TIMELESS LUXURY
AT THE WARRIOR HOTEL

Sioux City's newest hotel is also one of its oldest. The newly renovated and invigorated Warrior Hotel combines its original 1930 structure with the neighboring 1913 Davidson Building, creating an opulent getaway in the heart of downtown Sioux City. The 1930s Warrior Hotel was an Art Deco masterpiece by Kansas City architect Alonzo H. Gentry, full of elaborate stonework and metalwork. It was also full of interesting people. Sioux City, known as "Little Chicago" during the height of Prohibition, was a regular stop for gangsters—local legend even says that Al Capone once stayed at the Warrior (under a false name, of course!). The Warrior was the epitome of Siouxland luxury; its design was upscale, its ballrooms were grand, and it even had a barbershop! The new Warrior is a Marriott Autograph Collection hotel, combining all the best modern comforts and amenities with beautifully restored details from two buildings on the National Register of Historic Places. The modern hotel features a pool, its own bowling alley, a state-of-the-art fitness center, a relaxing spa, a gourmet restaurant, and even apartments—in case you really want to extend your stay.

525 Sixth St.
(712) 350-8875
TheWarriorHotel.com

85

ADMIRE ARCHITECTURE
AT THE WOODBURY COUNTY COURTHOUSE

The Woodbury County Courthouse is on the National Register of Historic Places for good reason! Designed and constructed by William Steele, a leading student of Frank Lloyd Wright, in 1917 and 1918, the courthouse is the world's largest public building designed in the uniquely Midwestern "Prairie School" architectural style. The courthouse interior includes exquisite stonework, murals, stained and leaded glass, many plaques, memorials, and historical artifacts, and even a fountain full of fish! The same marble worker created the faces of Mount Rushmore and the courthouse's interior stairs. Be sure to look up at the outside of the courthouse as well to admire the work of famed Italian American sculptor Alfonso Iannelli. But the Woodbury County Courthouse isn't merely an attraction for architecture pilgrims from around the globe—it's a working courthouse, filled with county offices and, yes, litigants, lawyers, and judges every day!

620 Douglas St.
(712) 279-6611
WoodburyCountyIowa.gov

HONOR HEROES
AT SIOUXLAND FREEDOM PARK

The Siouxland Freedom Park in South Sioux City, Nebraska, is a place for healing and for honoring memories. The centerpiece of the park is a half-scale replica of the Vietnam Veterans Memorial in Washington, DC. The park also features statues, a Freedom Rock painted by Ray "Bubba" Sorensen II, a dog park, and an interpretive center planned to include displays honoring veterans of each American war. One of Siouxland Freedom Park's major goals is to preserve and share the memories of veterans, so the interpretive center will include recordings of veterans' stories in their own words, as well as space for in-person events. The Siouxland Freedom Park hosts events for VFW and American Legion groups from Iowa, Nebraska, and South Dakota, as well as memorial events open to the general public.

1801 Veterans Dr.
South Sioux City, NE 68776
(402) 412-1776
SiouxlandFreedomPark.org

87

FOLLOW THE CAPTAINS
TO SPIRIT MOUND

According to legend, Spirit Mound, a large hill just outside Vermillion, South Dakota, is home to evil spirits who kill anyone who comes near. The Omaha, the Sioux, and the Otoe peoples all steered clear of Spirit Mound, and Native American residents of the area warned the Lewis and Clark Expedition to do the same, though Lewis and Clark ignored this advice and instead hiked to Spirit Mound's summit. Thereafter, Spirit Mound and its history were largely forgotten, until recent efforts began to restore the area to its condition at the time of the expedition. This effort includes a large-scale program to restore the native prairie. Today, visitors willing to risk the ire of the spirits can enjoy tallgrass prairie, interpretive signs, and modern restrooms, all while retracing the steps of the early explorers!

Highway 19 & 312th St.
Vermillion, SD 57069
SpiritMound.com

VENTURE INTO VERMILLION'S W. H. OVER MUSEUM

At the W. H. Over Museum in Vermillion, South Dakota, visitors learn the cultural and natural history of the Vermillion area. In the museum's Discovery Room, the curious of all ages can quench their thirst for hands-on experiences and information. Svetwold Hall, meanwhile, houses temporary exhibits and hosts special events with the help of its Pullman Kitchen. Highlights of the collection include preserved animals, including a bison and a bald eagle, intricate Native American beadwork, and antique farm implements. And if you want to take a piece of South Dakota history home with you, stop by the gift shop, where you'll find an extensive selection of beads and other Native American-made items!

1110 University St.
Vermillion, SD 57069
(605) 659-6151
WHOverMuseum.org

EXPERIENCE DAKOTA TERRITORIAL HISTORY
AT THE MEAD CULTURAL EDUCATION CENTER

The Mead Cultural Education Center in Yankton, South Dakota, was founded in 1879 as the Dakota Hospital for the Insane. The original hospital superintendent believed that beautiful surroundings might help the patients, and the building still features many original architectural touches, like a grand marble staircase and external walls of Sioux quartzite. Today's visitors can learn about the history of the Dakota territories, the hospital, and healthcare in South Dakota. The center also includes the Children's Transportation Museum, where young museumgoers are welcome to climb and play on a variety of vehicles, from a keelboat to early cars, to a wagon recreated from parts of several authentic 19th-century wooden wagons! The Mead is also known for one-of-a-kind events, including a masked costume ball for Mardi Gras, a spooky history tour each Halloween, and a Victorian Christmas celebration in December!

82 Mickelson Dr.
Yankton, SD 57078
(605) 665-3898
MeadBuilding.org

HIKE TO HISTORY
AT FIRST BRIDE'S GRAVE

At Ravine Park in the southern part of Sioux City, a short but steep hike in the woods leads to an unexpected surprise. Atop a bluff, you'll find the grave of the woman in the first recorded marriage in Sioux City: Rosalie Menard Leonais. Rosalie Menard married fur trader Joseph Leonais in a ceremony performed by a traveling priest in 1853, when she was about 15 years old. The couple eventually had four children, and Rosalie died at 27 shortly after the birth of her youngest, a boy named William. The Sioux City Pioneer Club built this memorial to Rosalie, called First Bride's Grave, in 1938, when Rosalie would have been 100 years old.

Ravine Park
Lincoln Way & S Lewis Blvd.

TIP
After hiking to First Bride's Grave, take the time to explore the other trails in Ravine Park, where you'll climb over fallen logs, walk down a steep ravine, and pass (carefully!) along a 30-foot loess cliff.

ALL ABOARD
AT THE SIOUX CITY RAILROAD MUSEUM

Sioux City was once a hub for the Milwaukee Railroad, and restoration efforts have transformed a former railroad workshop into a 32-acre museum dedicated to sharing everything locomotive. In the six-stall roundhouse, visitors can see, touch, and climb into real train engines like the Ironhorse, a massive 1924 steam locomotive that's on the National Register of Historic Places! Another visitor favorite is the model train building, with an elaborate 75-by-15-foot HO-scale model railroad display. The Sioux City Railroad Museum hosts some of the best holiday events in Siouxland, including Halloween at the Roundhouse and Santa's Whistlestop Tour, as well as children's story times, films, and lectures for all ages. One of the newer features at the museum is a 15-inch gauge grand-scale rideable train, one of fewer than 100 in the United States. So don your engineer caps (or buy a new one in the gift shop) and come ride, learn about, and celebrate trains, Siouxland style!

3400 Sioux River Rd.
(712) 233-6996
SiouxCityRailroadMuseum.org

Photo courtesy of George Lindblade

SHOPPING AND FASHION

CRUNCH SOME JOLLY TIME POPCORN

Get your popcorn fix at Jolly Time, the oldest popcorn company in America! Locally owned since its founding in 1914, Jolly Time Popcorn and its parent company, the American Popcorn Company, manufacture every kind of popcorn you can imagine. At the company's storefront in Sioux City, you can find dozens of flavors from Jolly Time's Koated Kernels line, like coconut caramel, raspberry cheesecake, the Koated Kernels Sioux City 50/50 mix of white cheddar and caramel, and Blast-O-Butter microwave popcorn. Popcorn lovers will also learn the long history of the American Popcorn Company and Jolly Time, and of popcorn more generally, at the store's mini-museum. Not sure what to buy? Try the free samples!

1717 Terminal Dr.
(712) 560-6973
KoatedKernels.com

FIND YOUR FANDOM
AT ACME COMICS

Acme Comics and Collectibles in Sioux City carries an extensive selection of comic books, toys, cards, artwork, and games from a wide variety of fandoms, including DC, Marvel, Harry Potter, and Disney. New comics come in on Wednesdays, and Acme has an extensive back catalog that customers can search through. Acme is also Siouxland's best place for in-store gaming, with regular evening sessions of Magic: The Gathering and Dungeons & Dragons. And don't miss Acme's special events, from mini-cons, to miniature painting workshops, to comic-drawing sessions with top industry names. Worth a special mention are the nationwide Free Comic Book Day every May and Acme's tradition of handing out free comics at its annual Halloween event—both of which feature kid-friendly costumed characters of every kind, from armored knights to *Star Wars* stormtroopers.

1622 Pierce St.
(712) 258-6171
AcmeFirst.net

SWEETEN YOUR DAY
AT PALMER'S CANDY

Palmer's Candy Company has been making delicious treats in Siouxland since 1878, and the best place to taste those treats is at Palmer's Old Tyme Candy Shoppe. Inside this old-fashioned candy store, you'll find shelves of prepackaged candy and bulk bins stuffed with cherry sours, dipped pretzels, almonds and peanuts covered in delicious dark chocolate, and more. There's also a bakery case full of truffles, fudge, and other small-batch delights. But the Old Tyme Candy Shoppe has more than just candy. In one corner of the store, you'll find Siouxland's best selection of artisanal dry goods, including cheese, jam, pasta, and spreads. Another corner holds a mini-museum displaying antique candy-making equipment and information about Palmer's history. The precise selection of candy frequently changes, with a rotating variety of seasonal treats and factory seconds. But you'll always find Palmer's signature candy bar: the Twin Bing, two round, cherry-flavored nougats covered in chocolate and mixed with chopped peanuts!

405 Wesley Parkway
(712) 258-7790
PalmerCandy.com

95

CROSS THE MOAT
TO THINKER TOYS

In a silvery-gray castle, over a drawbridge that spans a rocky moat, you'll find Siouxland's best toy store: Thinker Toys. Inside the eastern half of the castle is a two-story, toy-filled wonderland where kites dangle overhead and huge plush friends wait for hugs. On the first floor of the front left tower is a train room with a play table, where you can find Brio, Thomas the Tank Engine, and Dinosaur Train. The tower's entire second floor is a LEGO room! The selection of playthings here is extensive, including Corolle dolls, PLAYMOBIL, Safari and Schleich miniatures, puppets, marbles, magic gear, prank kits, and board games—much of which you won't find at any big-box store. There's also a charming little vintage carousel near the entrance that toddlers and preschoolers can ride for a quarter! The western half of Thinker Toys contains the Castle Pub, with a separate entrance and an expansive selection of pizza and beer.

4400 Singing Hills Blvd.
(712) 271-8697
Facebook.com/ThinkerToys

AIM FOR BRIAR AND BOW

Channel your inner Robin Hood at Briar and Bow Archery, just east of Sioux City! Part sporting goods store, part indoor and outdoor archery range, when it comes to archery, Briar and Bow has you covered! The shop carries bows, arrowheads, strings, and targets from top brands like Bear, Easton, Hoyt, Morrell, Grim Reaper, New Archery, and Phantom. Arrows are built on the premises to user specifications, and fletching and repair services are also available. Briar and Bow offers lessons for all ages and hosts archery tournaments and other special events. One of the most unique aspects of this establishment is its variety of ranges—Briar and Bow has indoor 10-, 15-, and 20-yard ranges, and an outdoor walk-around range with ground-level and elevated shooting positions. The outdoor range is free to use!

1913 Highway 20
Lawton, IA 51030
(712) 255-5132
BriarAndBow.com

TIP
Briar and Bow is behind Midwest Auto of Siouxland, about five minutes past Menards on Highway 20.

97

BUY SOME BLING
AT THORPE AND COMPANY

Since 1900, Thorpe and Company has been selling some of Siouxland's best jewelry from its location in downtown Sioux City. The business has been a member of the American Gem Society (AGS) since the 1930s, and one of its jewelers was in the AGS's first graduating class! Thorpe and Company focuses on service and makes unique pieces to suit each customer with the help of on-site goldsmithing, an AGS lab, appraisal services, and laser engraving. The owners are as serious about ethical obligations as about jewelry, selling only cruelty-free diamonds and supporting charitable causes throughout Siouxland. Thorpe and Company also offers repair services and buys pre-owned fine jewelry. The store's reputation for excellence makes it no surprise that they are frequently nominated for and chosen as winners of awards, including the 2020 Siouxland Choice Award for best jewelry store in Siouxland!

501 Fourth St.
(712) 258-7501
ThorpeJewelers.com

FIND IT ALL
AT THE MARKETPLACE ON HAMILTON

On Hamilton Boulevard, Sioux City's busiest street, you'll find a row of some of Sioux City's best local shops. Heart and Hand Dry Goods is a quilter's paradise, with everything from reproductions of Civil War-era prints to the hottest modern designs, plus an impressive selection of gifts and regular quilting classes. E & Co. Clothing Boutique is an upscale clothing and gift boutique named after the owner's mother, Evie, whom many in Siouxland know for her chain of Evie's Hallmark stores (including the store two doors down). E & Co. offers the latest trends with a casual Midwest vibe, including some brands you won't find at any other store in the area. Book People is Sioux City's premier locally owned independent bookstore, with the latest bestsellers, beautiful gift books, a large children's selection, and dedicated shelving for authors from the Midwest. Hamilton Plaza also features Iowa-based grocery store Hy-Vee, Coney Island Wiener House, locally owned Wilmes Do It Best Hardware, and Minerva's, a great spot for locally owned fine dining.

Heart and Hand Dry Goods Company
3011 Hamilton Blvd.
(712) 258-3161
HeartAndHand.com

E & Co. Boutique
2919 Hamilton Blvd.
(712) 234-0090
Facebook.com/EandCoBoutique

Book People
2923 Hamilton Blvd.
(712) 258-1471
BookPeopleSC.Indilite.org

Evie's Hallmark
2931 Hamilton Blvd.
(712) 258-3453

Wilmes Do It Best Hardware
3049 Hamilton Blvd.
(712) 252-5176
WilmesHardware.DoItBest.com

STROLL THROUGH YANKTON'S MERIDIAN DISTRICT

The Meridian District in downtown Yankton, South Dakota, is the place to go for boutique shopping. Cute stores and dining combine with the Market at the Meridian farmers market, as well as frequent community festivals and special events, to make visiting the Meridian District a must! One shop that especially shines is furniture store River City Relics, which features everything from mid-century modern to trendy farmhouse chic, including many pieces made with beautifully reclaimed wood, all sold with tons of charm on the side. And don't miss the Meridian Bridge—this double-decker across the Missouri River was originally designed for rail traffic below and autos above, but is now converted entirely to a unique pedestrian bridge.

From Lynn Street to Burleigh Street,
between Fifth Street and the Missouri River
Yankton, SD 57078
Meridian-District.com

River City Relics
217 E Third St.
Yankton, SD 57078

100

SHOP LOCAL
AT SIOUX CITY GIFTS

Sioux City Gifts is both a store and a photography studio, with one-of-a-kind Siouxland flavor. The back room is the work space of the incomparable George Lindblade, a local legend widely viewed as Siouxland's best photographer. Lindblade and his wife opened Sioux City Gifts in the front half of the space to sell his work, along with the best products made here in Siouxland and fair-trade goods from around the world. Come and find souvenir T-shirts, jewelry, home decor, and an extensive selection of books by Siouxland writers. They also feature wonderful gift baskets full of local treats. Sioux City Gifts is itself a gift to all Siouxlanders and guests, and you won't find a better one-stop shop to experience what Siouxland has to offer!

1922 Pierce St.
(712) 255-4346
SiouxCityGifts.com

SUGGESTED ITINERARIES

DOWNTOWN DATE NIGHT

Sing the Blues and Eat Your Greens at the Blue Cafe, 13

Enjoy Historic Nightlife on Fourth Street, 28

Try Your Luck at the Hard Rock Hotel and Casino, 34

Savor the Sioux City Symphony Orchestra, 36

Stay in Timeless Luxury at the Warrior Hotel, 114

FAMILY FUN

Scream for Blue Bunny Ice Cream, 8

Enjoy Inclusive Play at Miracle Field, 70

Burrow Like a Badger at the Dorothy Pecaut Nature Center, 79

Play All Day at LaunchPad Children's Museum, 102

Sweeten Your Day at Palmer's Candy, 126

Cross the Moat to Thinker Toys, 127

UPSTREAM TO YANKTON & VERMILLION

Taste the Wagyu Beef at Red Steakhouse, 12

Get a Song Stuck in Your Head at the National Music Museum, 47

See What's Fishy at Gavins Point, 86

Follow the Captains to Spirit Mound, 117

Venture into Vermillion's W. H. Over Museum, 118

Experience Dakota Territorial History at the Mead Cultural Education Center, 119

Stroll Through Yankton's Meridian District, 132

ICE CREAM & TULIPS

Scream for Blue Bunny Ice Cream, 8

Gobble Down Flavor at the Iowa BBQ Company, 9

Go Dutch in Orange City, 14

Enjoy the Classics at the Le Mars Community Theatre, 39

Twirl Around Windmill Park and the Orange City Tulip Festival, 94

Pop into a Cute Little Museum, 96

RIVERFRONT HISTORY

Stroll Along America's Longest River, 54

Buzz by Bruguier Cabin, 91

Navigate to the Sergeant Floyd River Museum and Welcome Center, 99

Take an Expedition to the Lewis and Clark Interpretive Center, 103

SELFIE READY

Pick Your Own Fun, 6

Sing the Blues and Eat Your Greens at the Blue Cafe, 13

Indulge Your Sweet Tooth at the Sugar Shack, 23

Enjoy Historic Nightlife on Fourth Street, 28

Twirl Around Windmill Park and the Orange City Tulip Festival, 94

Be a Connoisseur at the Sioux City Art Center, 110

ACTIVITIES
BY SEASON

SPRING

Pick Your Own Fun, 6

See the City from Grandview Park, 44

Take Me Out to a Sioux City Explorers Ballgame, 62

Watch the Best at the NAIA Championships, 67

Toss the Pigskin with Stampede and Bandits Football, 76

Twirl Around Windmill Park and the Orange City Tulip Festival, 94

SUMMER

Scream for Blue Bunny Ice Cream, 8

Sing Along with a Sioux City Municipal Band, 40

See the City from Grandview Park, 44

Make a Splash at Siouxland Pools, 56

Take Me Out to the Sioux City Explorers Ballgame, 62

Buzz by Bruguier Cabin, 91

FALL

Pick Your Own Fun, 6
Watch the Best at the NAIA Championships, 67
Toss the Pigskin with Stampede and Bandits Football, 76
Hike More Loess at Stone State Park, 78
All Aboard at the Sioux City Railroad Museum, 121

WINTER

Enjoy Historic Nightlife on Fourth Street, 28
Savor the Sioux City Symphony Orchestra, 36
Glide Downhill at Cone Park, 57
Check (Out) the Sioux City Musketeers, 82
Rise Above It All in the Sioux City Skywalk System, 112
All Aboard at the Sioux City Railroad Museum, 121

INDEX

1008 Key Club, 29
Acme Comics, 125
Adams Homestead Nature Preserve, 74
Anderson Dance Pavilion, 54, 98
Andy's Sweet Tooth, 93
Angel De Cora Museum and Research Center, 96, 97
Archie's Waeside, 24, 25
Art SUX Gallery, 113
Autumn Grove Apple Orchard, 6, 7
Bandits (arena football team), 41, 76, 139, 140
Bigelow Park, 84
Billy Boy, 4, 43
Blue Cafe, 13, 135, 137
Blue Cat Gallery, 95
Bob's Drive Inn, 31
Book People, 130, 131
Brad's Breads, 14
Briar and Bow, 128
Brightside, 29
Brown's Lake, 84
Browns, The, 48
Bruguier Cabin, 91
Buffalo Alice, 29
Calliope Village, 92
Century Home, 96, 97
Century Theater, 48
Clay County Fair, 51
Cone Park, 57, 140
Coney Island Wiener House, 130
Crystal Cove (disc golf course), 59
Dakota Dunes Country Club, 64
Dakota Territorial History Museum, 119
Dakota/Thurston Fair, 51

Danish Alps, 61
Diamond Thai, 16
Diving Elk, 29
Dorothy Pecaut Nature Center, 4, 79, 135
DropZone, 60
Dutch Bakery, 14, 15
E & Co., 130, 131
El Fredo, 18, 19
Evie's Hallmark, 130, 131
First Bride's Grave, 120
Five Ridge Prairie Preserve, 85
Flight 232 Memorial, 54, 98, 104
Fred G. Dale Planetarium, 75
Freedom Park, 116
Gavins Point Dam, 86
Gavins Point National Fish Hatchery & Aquarium, 86, 135
Golden Pheasant, 24, 25
Grandview Park, 40, 44, 45, 58, 59, 139
Hard Rock Hotel & Casino, 34
Hardline Coffee Co., 11
Heart and Hand Dry Goods, 130, 131
Highway 20, 10, 93, 128
Hillview Recreation Area, 59
Hy-Vee, 130
IBP Ice Center, 68
Iowa BBQ Co., 9
Jerry's, 18, 19
Jitters, 2
Jolly Time, 124
Kahill's, 24, 25
Koffie Knechtion, 11
La Juanita, 17
Lamb Arts Regional Theater, 35
LaunchPad Children's Museum, 102, 135
Lawton Exchange, 24, 25
Leif Erickson Park, 68, 69
Le Mars Community Theater, 39

Lewis & Clark Interpretive Center and Betty Strong Encounter Center, 54
Lewis & Clark Theatre Company, 46
Lindblade, George, 105, 133
Lindsay's Flower Patch, 6, 7
Little White Store, 14, 15
Loess Hills Scenic Byway, 85
Long Lines Family Recreation Center, 66
M's on Fourth, 21
Marketplace on Hamilton, 130
Marquee, 29, 38
Marto Brewing Company, 29
Mead Cultural Education Center, 119, 135
Mental Health Institute, 58, 59
MercyOne Hospital, 113
Meridian Bridge, 132
Meridian District, 132, 136
Mid America Museum of Aviation & Transportation, 104
Miles Inn, 30, 31
Milwaukee Railroad, 20, 121
Milwaukee Wiener House, 20
Miracle Field, 56, 70, 71, 135
Missouri River, 24, 54, 56, 74, 81, 84, 86, 87, 90, 98, 99, 100, 132
Movillatte, 10, 11
Musketeers (hockey team), 41, 82, 140
NAIA Women's Basketball Championships, 67
National Music Museum, 47, 135
New Stage Players, 49
Norm Waitt Sr. YMCA, 56
North Forty, 64
Orpheum Theatre, 36, 37, 112, 113
Palmer's Old Tyme Candy Shoppe, 126
Park Jefferson International Speedway, 55
Peirce Mansion, 106, 107
Pierce Street Coffee Works, 10, 11
Pizza Ranch, 27
Plymouth County Fair, 51
Plymouth County Museum, 96, 97

Ponca State Park, 81
Postal Playhouse, 39
Promenade (movie theater), 28, 29
Ravine Park, 120
Rebo's, 29
Red Steakhouse, 12, 135
Rev-Tac, 80
River City Relics, 132
Riverside Park (disc golf course), 4, 42, 56, 70, 71, 91
Roadside Park, 59
Rockestra, 38
Rollerama, 72
Rush Werks, 73
Saturday in the Park, 45
Scarecrow Farm, 6, 7
Sentinels of the Prairie, 93
Sergeant Bluff Historical Museum, 97
Sergeant Floyd Monument, x, 100
Sergeant Floyd River Museum and Welcome Center, 99
Sertoma Park, 57, 69
Sioux City Art Center, 110, 111, 137
Sioux City City Hall, 105
Sioux City Community Theatre, 4, 42
Sioux City Conservatory of Music, 13
Sioux City Convention Center, 113
Sioux City Farmers Market, 6, 7
Sioux City Gifts, 133
Sioux City Municipal Band, 40, 139
Sioux City Police Museum, 105
Sioux City Public Library, 113
Sioux City Public Museum, 28, 104, 106, 108
Sioux City Railroad Museum, 4, 121, 140
Sioux City Symphony Orchestra, 36, 135, 140
Siouxland Freedom Park, 116
Siouxnami Waterpark, 56
Skywalk System, 112, 140
Sneaky's, 22

Snyder Bend, 84
Soho Kitchen, 29
Southwood Conservation Area, 83
Special Teas, 5
Spirit Mound, 117, 136
Stampede (football team), 76, 77, 139, 140
Stone Bru, 10, 11
Stone State Park, 78, 140
Sugar Shack, 23, 137
Sunken Garden Park, 107
Sunkist, 2, 3
Sweetwater Cafe, 113
Table 32, 24, 25
Tastee Inn & Out, 31
Thinker Toys, 127, 135
Thorpe and Company, 129
Trinity Heights, 109
Tripp Park, 69
Tulip Festival, 94
Tyson Events Center, 6, 41, 66, 67, 76, 82
Udder Delights, 26
Union County Historical Society, 96
W. H. Over Museum, 118, 136
War Eagle, 90, 91
Warrior Hotel, 114, 135
Wayne Chicken Show, 95
Wayne Planetarium (see Fred G. Dale Planetarium)
Wells Visitor Center & Ice Cream Parlor, 8
West Floyd Park, 59
Windmill Park, 94, 136, 137, 139
Woodbury County Courthouse, 115
Woodbury County Fairgrounds, 50
Yankton Ice Rink, 68, 69